NEWCASTLE-UNDER-LYME PUBS

MERVYN EDWARDS

AMBERLEY

First published 2016

Amberley Publishing
The Hill, Stroud
Gloucestershire, GL5 4EP

www.amberley-books.com

Copyright © Mervyn Edwards, 2016

The right of Mervyn Edwards to be identified
as the Author of this work has been asserted in
accordance with the Copyrights, Designs and
Patents Act 1988.

ISBN 978 1 4456 5849 0 (print)
ISBN 978 1 4456 5850 6 (ebook)

British Library Cataloguing in Publication Data.
A catalogue record for this book is available from
the British Library.

Typesetting by Amberley Publishing.
Printed in the UK.

Contents

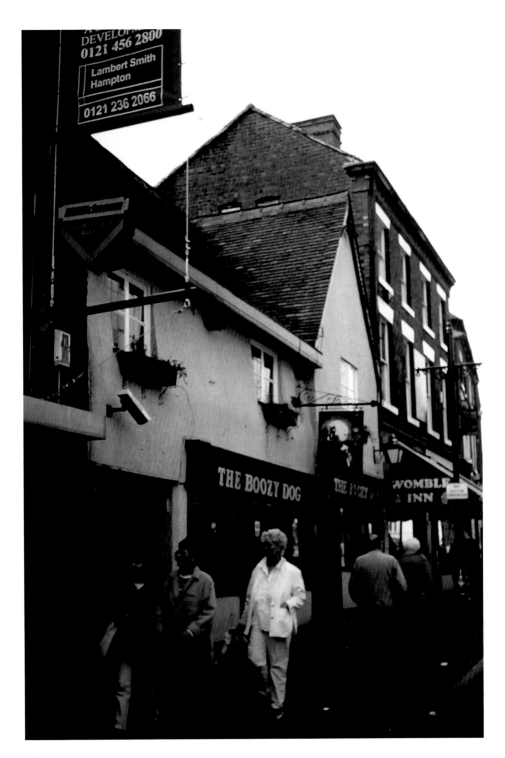

The Boozy Dog.

Preface

This book is a follow-up to *Stoke-on-Trent Pubs*, published by Amberley Publishing in 2014, and is constructed along similar lines. It is a gazetteer-style work that offers pocket histories of selected pubs in the Borough of Newcastle-under-Lyme. As with *Stoke-on-Trent Pubs*, the question was which pubs to include. The final selection had nothing to do with my affiliation with the local branch of CAMRA (the Campaign for Real Ale), nor any loyalties I may have to certain Newcastle pubs – insofar as I have any.

The choice of outlets in this book is made in the interest of featuring pubs with disparate stories, embracing old coaching inns, former beerhouses, hotel-style establishments, town centre pubs or backstreet locals. The editors at Amberley also had their say in the matter and we believed that it would add variety to feature a few borough pubs within easy walking distance of the town itself – thus, pubs in nearby villages have made our final cut, and they often offer different narratives. Inclusion in this book is not necessarily an endorsement of a pub's merit, nor is its exclusion to be taken of an indication of a hostelry's failings.

Having left Wolstanton Grammar School at the age of eighteen, my first regular watering hole was the Victoria in May Bank – though I didn't become what I would describe as a drinker until I was around twenty-one. Over the years, I've seen many marvellous boozers either significantly reinvented, closed or demolished. The radical refurbishment of the three-rooms-and-a-passage Boat & Horses in 1999 was particularly painful. It was gutted – which was exactly how I felt about the loss of the erstwhile floor plan. Some pubs have been converted for alternative use, such as Ye Olde Merlin Tavern in Church Street, the Bear on West Brampton and the John O'Gaunt on Silverdale Road, some have been given fatuous names and many have been demolished. In the latter category, we find establishments such as the Smithfield (2006), the Sutherland Arms (2006), the Hanging Gate/Castle Tavern (2009) and the Pool Dam (2010).

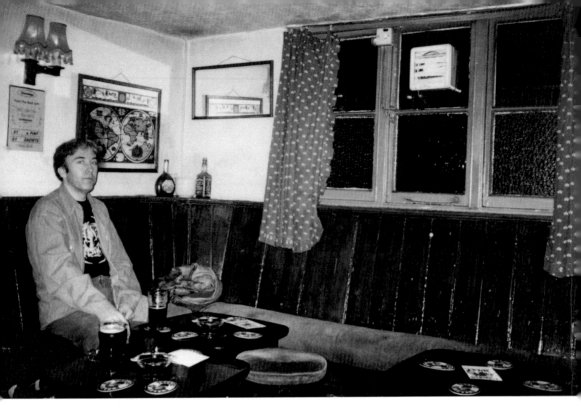

Above: Boat & Horses, 15 January 1997. Cliff Proctor drinks in the Snug.

Below: Boat & Horses, 1 May 1997.

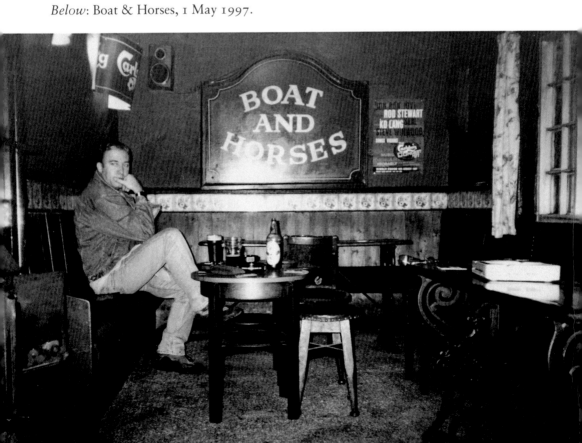

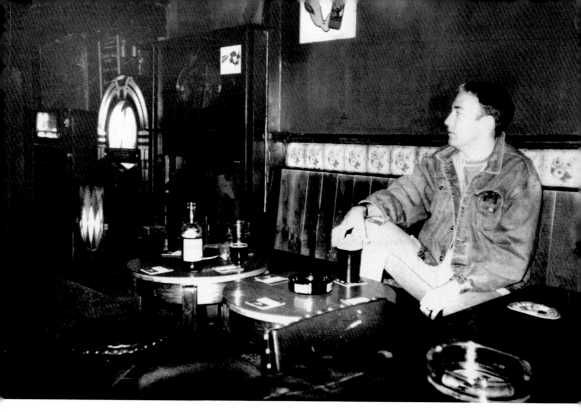

Above: Boat & Horses, 1 May 1997.

Below: Boat & Horses, 24 March 1998.

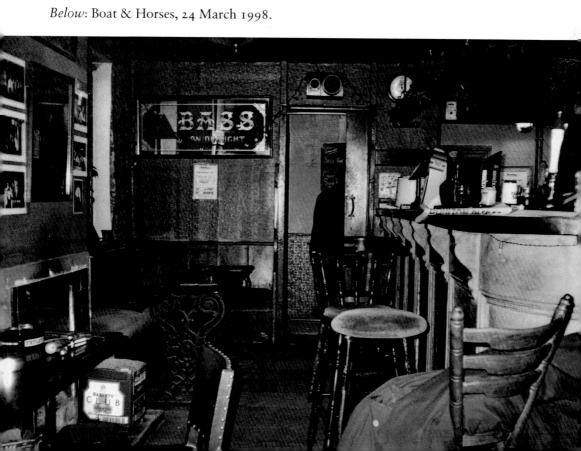

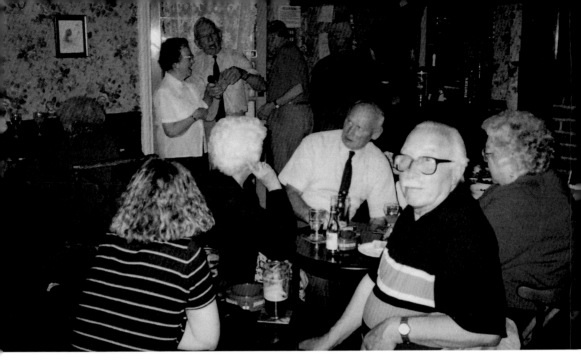

Above: The Bear, 6 May 2000. Ida and Harry Keeling are singing over the microphone while Ken Smith sits in the foreground.

Below: The John O'Gaunt, 29 July 2013. This pub was known as the Castle between 1999 and 2013, when it reverted to its traditional name.

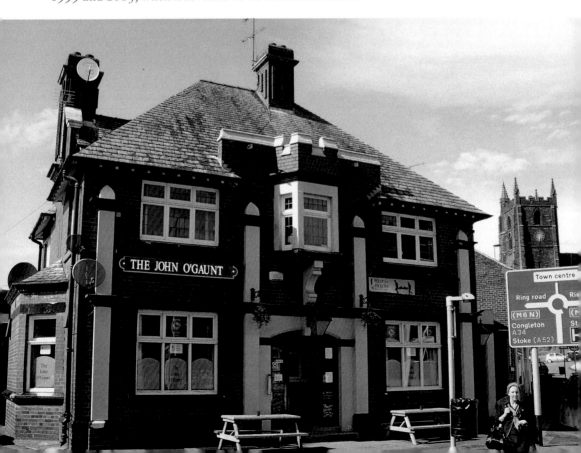

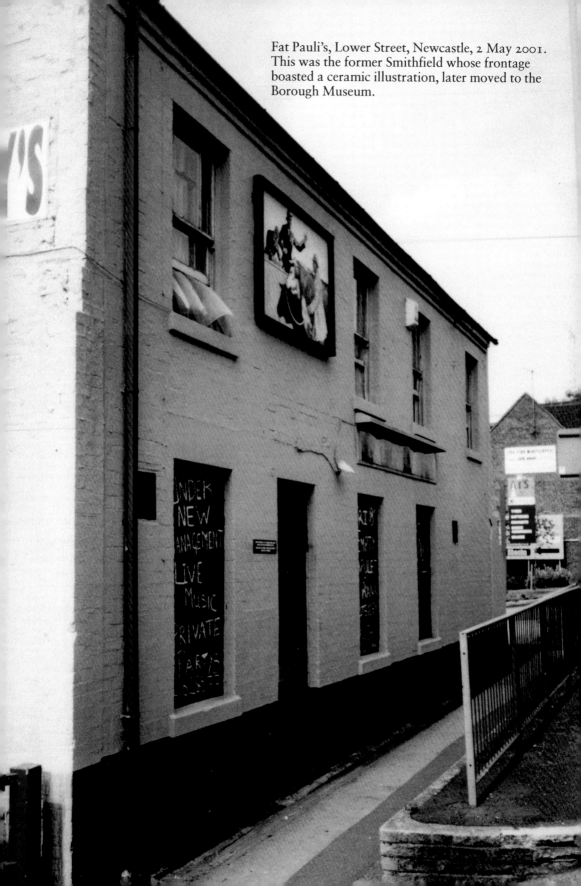

Fat Pauli's, Lower Street, Newcastle, 2 May 2001.
This was the former Smithfield whose frontage
boasted a ceramic illustration, later moved to the
Borough Museum.

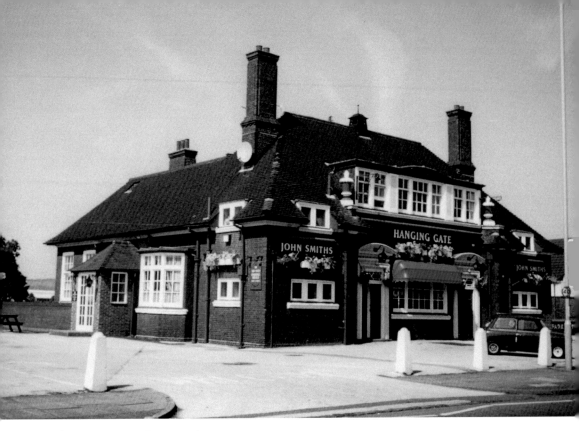

Above: Hanging Gate, 20 August 1991.

Below: The Castle Tavern, 20 April 2003.

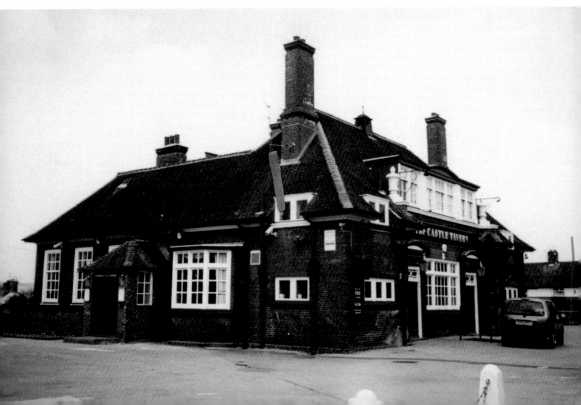

They've all been memorials to someone or other's misspent youth, but the beauty of the pubs featured in the main directory of this short volume is that all of them were still trading at the time of writing. Let's hope that I am not featuring them again twenty years from now in a book called Lost Pubs of Newcastle!

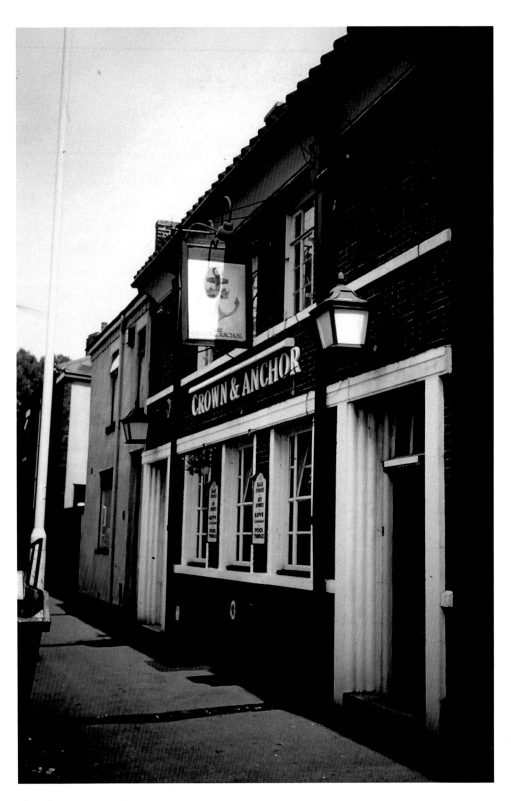

The Crown & Anchor.

The Pubs

It wasn't that long ago that Newcastle was being dubbed the 'Bar Capital of North Staffordshire'. It offered a nocturnal festival of brightly lit pleasure palaces that vied with each other for the custom of those with a high disposable income, or those who – temporarily feeling 'flush' – just wished to banish their weekday cares in a hedonistic orgy of drink, dance, dining or drugs, much to the disapproval of certain sections of society.

New watering holes seemed to open every other month and the local press focused regularly on policing issues and the detrimental effect on other business premises that were being shunned by daytime shoppers in favour of the more vibrant retail attractions of Hanley. Boarded-up shops in Newcastle told their own story. Newcastle was unable to compete with the city centre, but its mushrooming bar culture did enable it to give Hanley a run for its money. In March 1998, *The Sentinel* referred to thirty-plus bars, bistros and other night spots then flexing muscle in the town, naming Viva Bar, Bar Indigo, the Bull's Head, the Farrow and Firkin, Blues Bar, Edwards', the Golden Lion, Pablo Frankie, the Albion, Brassington's, Azzuri, the Black Friar and Pinocchio's. Many of Newcastle's style-over-substance outlets faded into oblivion, or changed to embrace the latest fad, adopting some other abstruse name. Some fell foul of the police. One retailer lamented, 'The shops are disappearing and you can't walk around at night for drunken clowns.'

The eddying patterns of history tell us that nothing really changes. Town developments wax and wane, shimmering in and out of our view like the gaudy frontage of a newfangled bar, viewed by some squinty-eyed, inebriated reveller. Newcastle's historic Guildhall became a bar in 1999, triggering criticisms that the borough council was selling off the 'family silver'. In 2008, it was transformed into a council customer services centre, to the approval of many commentators. The town's post office building became a Wetherspoon's pub in 2002. The Yorkshire Bank building in Ironmarket was

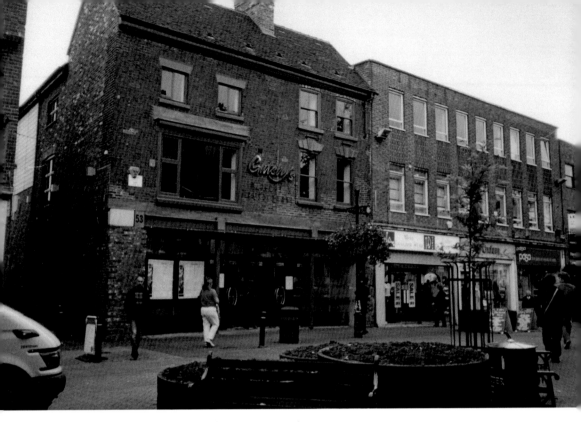

The former Gatsby's, Ironmarket, 28 September 2004.

transformed into Gatsby's wine bar and restaurant, only to close, reopen, and close again.

'Twas ever thus. If we turn back the pages of history, we find that social changes and town planning by turns created and destroyed pubs. The slum clearance schemes in Newcastle in the 1960s and the council's determination to make it a modern, 'destination' shopping town put paid to no end of pubs in the helter-skelter rush to embrace the future. The Clarence, the Red Lion and the Lamb Inn were among those that disappeared during this period.

However, Newcastle had been the bar capital of North Staffordshire long before, and for the reasons why, we must look at its distant past.

Various eighteenth-century documents and directories refer to 'Newcastle-under-Lyme and neighbourhood' – effectively viewing the Potteries as a mere satellite of Newcastle. Newcastle was a metropolis for the conurbation, on account of its crucial location on the arterial road running from London to Carlisle, the great road north that served those centres at the forefront of the Industrial Revolution. It was the post road, and mail for the Potteries was distributed from Newcastle, the postal centre for the area. The turnpiking of the Tittensor to Talke section of the great road north in 1714 consolidated Newcastle's position as the capital of the district, boosting its mercantile growth

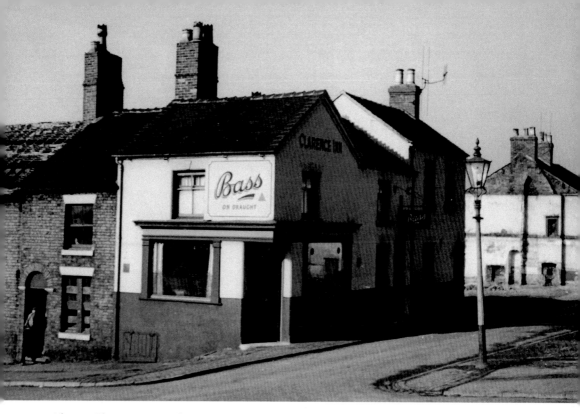

Above: Clarence Inn, Clarence Street, *c.* 1958. (Courtesy Paul Niblett)

Below: King's Head, Penkhull Street, later High Street. Date unknown.

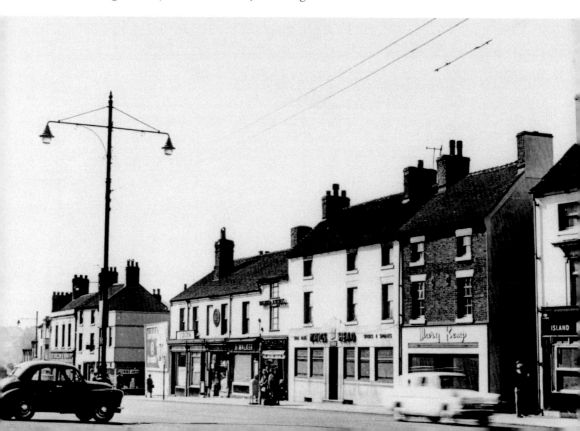

and its development as a coaching stop. Once people had arrived in the town, they required accommodation, refreshment and entertainment. Newcastle's inns mushroomed. The (New) Roebuck, the Talbot, the Three Tuns, the King's Head, the Globe Hotel and, later, the Castle Hotel were among the coaching or posting houses.

Visitors came from a distance to enjoy the entertainment in the town, which could boast of its Newcastle and Pottery Theatre by 1788. The nearby Shakespeare Hotel often offered concomitant amusements in the way of cockfighting, patronised by gentlemen from Cheshire and Derbyshire. Its favourable location and amenities were promoted in the local newspapers of July 1802:

> TO BE LET And entered upon immediately, or at Michaelmas next, THE SHAKESPEARE TAVERN, in the Borough of Newcastle-under-Lyme, Staffordshire.
>
> This house is pleasantly situated and fronts to the south, at the end of the town, at the junction of three great roads leading into the Staffordshire Potteries, and is also adjoining the theatre.
>
> The Tavern is extensive and convenient, with an elegant and very large Assembly Room attached to it, also a good Brewhouse, Stables, Coach-house, and a large Cock-pit with two feeding rooms adjoining …

Entertainment in Newcastle pubs was nothing if not diverse. In 1870, it was announced that the extraordinary gymnast known as 'the African Blondin' had shown his great dexterity on a 40-foot-high rope suspended above the yard at the back of the Roebuck. The Fox & Goose staged music hall entertainments, advertising the Great Kentish Giant – he was apparently 7 feet 4 inches – in 1856. The Cock Inn not only had a music hall attached but a skittle alley and rifle gallery.

The market town of Newcastle was a great centre for trade and the fairs were occasions when commercial activity and the amusement of visitors could be combined. Newcastle could boast of seven fairs and six cattle fairs by 1840. In 1838, the Star in Ironmarket was advertised to be sold by auction, being 'in the centre of the Butchers' Market'. It had, for several years, 'done considerable business, particularly as a market house' and had piggeries attached. Pubs were connected in all manner of ways with the town's status as an agricultural centre. A large pig was exhibited at the Red Bull in George Street in 1842, and a 'fat pig to be shot for' was advertised by the Sutherland Arms in 1866. In 1871, a Smithfield cattle market was laid out in Blackfriars Road, hence the name of the Smithfield pub in Lower Street, formerly the Leopard – it served local farmers. A ceramic pub sign depicting a bull, auctioneer and a clerk, was

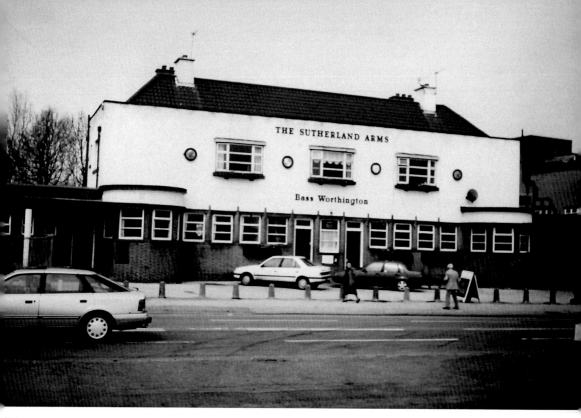

The Sutherland Arms, 18 April 1994.

removed from the front of the Smithfield, upon its demolition in 2006 and removed to the Borough Museum and Art Gallery.

Newcastle pubs played host to numerous clubs and organisations. The Lodge of Moderns – who were freemasons – was established at the Crown Inn in 1767. Lodges of the Independent Order of Oddfellows were meeting at the Sutherland Arms in the 1840s, while a meeting of bricklayers interested in inaugurating a branch lodge of the Operative Bricklayers Society of London convened at the Fountain Inn on Fletcher Street in 1864.

Sporting clubs were attached to some pubs, with the Newcastle and Pottery Rifle Club gathering at the Castle Hotel by the 1850s. Newcastle Swifts Football Club and the Newcastle cycling club met at the Cheshire Cheese in the 1890s. The relationship between pubs and politics triggered much bribery and corruption, with one leading citizen bragging, in 1902, that he could buy hundreds of votes at 1½d each – the price of a pint of beer. Drink truly lubricated every aspect of Newcastle society.

Trade directories reveal the full picture of the pub's dominance in Newcastle. The *Newcastle and Pottery General Commercial Directory* (1822–23) lists sixty-two individuals connected with the drink trade, including John Greaves, the maltster and victualler who kept the Queens at Basford. The list includes

Important Notice to the Bricklayers of Newcastle-under-Lyme, and Vicinity.

A MEETING of the BRICKLAYERS

Of the above place will be held on TUESDAY EVENING, FEBRUARY 23, 1864, at the

"FOUNTAIN INN." Fletcher Street, Newcastle-under-Lyme,

For the purpose of *inaugurating* a Branch Lodge of the OPERATIVE BRICKLAYERS' SOCIETY of London. The advantages from such an Association are felt by all who follow the calling of a Bricklayer, it gives to men a special character, and is a source of strength ; it keeps them compact, and enables them to concentrate their efforts to one end ; for singly we are weak and exercise no influence on rabid and sensual men ; therefore, where there is unity of interest, let there be unity of support, and the day is not far distant when you will enjoy the full fruits of your labour.

Members will be enrolled at the low entrance fee of 2s. 6d. **The Benefits of the Society are :**—Funeral Allowance £8 ; at Wife's Death £6 ; and 1s. Travelling Relief when in Search of Employment ; and the protection of the Society—all for 3d. per week, which sum would have to be paid weekly for Funeral Money to any Insurance Society in the United Kingdom, let alone other benefits you would receive.

Delegates from the District Lodges will attend with Books, Rules, &c., so as to see the Lodge opened and established We hope our fellow-workmen will rally round and greet them with a hearty welcome, for no progress can be made without united action.

NOTICE.—An enrolled Sick Fund attached to this Society. Any member desirous of joining it, from 16 to 45 years of age will on payment of 3d. per week, insure 10s. per week in Sickness ; 4½d. will insure 15s. per week in Sickness.

Chair taken at Eight o'Clock.

E. COULSON, *Gen. Sec.*

Fountain Inn, Fletcher Street. This 1864 notice was for the attention of the bricklaying profession.

fifty-three specifically named hostelries and also reminds us that some landlords had the safety net of a second profession. For instance, Joseph Allen at the Black Trumpeter was a stonemason working with marble stone; John Allport at the Star was a butcher; John Bloor at the Lamb was a clockmaker; Andrew Bristol at the Woolpack was a plumber and glazier; William Cooper at the Red Lion was a saddler; Edward Lowe at the Queen's Head was a hairdresser; Samuel Mellard at the Red Lion was a cordwainer; and John Wood at the King's Arms was a common stage carrier. Thus, we see how publicans had multifarious connections with the wider trade of the town.

The Beer Act of 1830 was to have a significant impact on the increase of watering holes across the nation and the story in Newcastle was no different. *Cottrill's Police Directory* (1836) lists sixty-four taverns and public houses and thirty-nine beerhouses. White (1851) gives sixty-one inns and taverns and thirty-five beerhouses. Even as late as 1940, *Kelly's Directory* lists sixty-one public houses and inns, though eighteen were beer retailers only, and five hotels.

The role of the public house in Newcastle – as elsewhere – changed in the interwar period, prompted by a reaction against Victorian architecture, the rise of the 'improved pub' and the desire for 'fewer and better' hostelries that catered more readily for families and those visitors in motor cars. This was

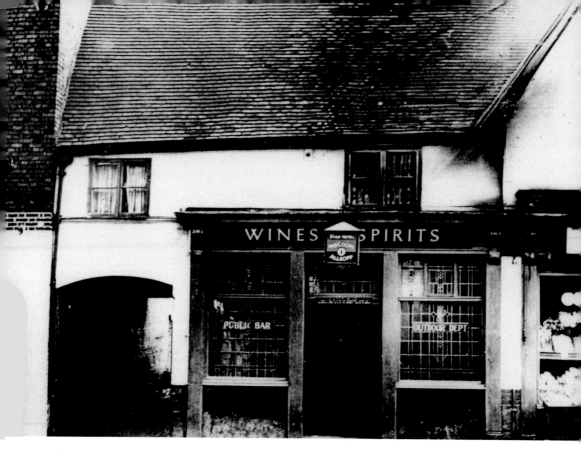

Above: Star, Ironmarket. Date unknown.

Below: The Hempstalls from St Michael's Road, 23 June 1998.

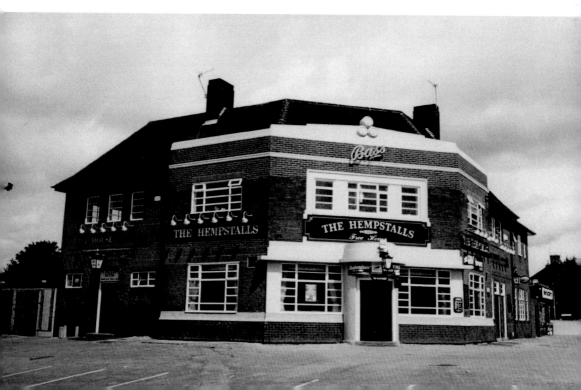

the period that saw the rebuilding of the Hanging Gate (*c.* 1930), the John O'Gaunt (1934) and the building of pubs on new estates such as the Hempstalls Inn (1936).

Around this time, a popular saying had it that you could 'stand on the Central pavement, playing with a Golden Ball, eating Cheshire Cheese, and having a sip of Old Vine, and watching the Rising Sun, setting on the Globe, which weighed Three Tuns'. In this way Newcastilians acknowledged a few of the wealth of pubs in Newcastle, while simultaneously paying homage to the town's proud pub history.

However, from the late 1950s, the pub scene in Newcastle would change forever. Newcastle had always been ready to peddle its history, but now there came a belly-to-the-ground rush to embrace a sequinned, prosperous future. There were many reasons for this: supermarkets and chain stores were usurping the custom formerly enjoyed by independents and family businesses – old shops, old houses and old pubs were not easily adaptable for modern needs. Crucially, the opening of the M6 motorway through Cheshire in 1963 reduced much of the long-distance traffic through the High Street stretch of the A34 in

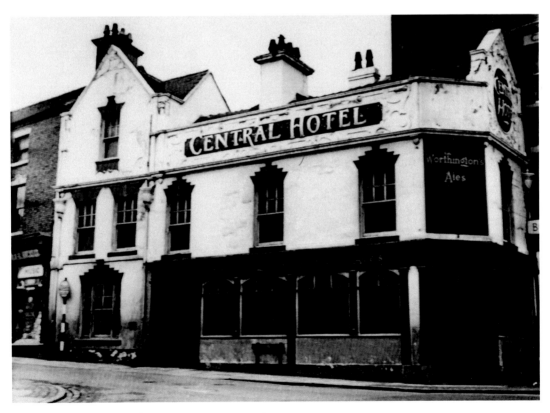

Central Hotel, Red Lion Square. Date unknown.

Newcastle. However, traffic congestion in the town centre remained a problem and it was claimed that it was killing the trade in High Street, where shoppers patronised the open-air markets in the closest proximity to the through traffic.

Within a few years, this heavy traffic would be taken out of the town centre and onto the new bypass. This offered the council a chance to redevelop shops with the aim of establishing Newcastle as a district shopping centre. However, the improvements necessitated much demolition and many pubs bit the dust in a decade of much upheaval.

Red Lion Square changed drastically in the 1960s, not least because three public houses were demolished. The Hind's Vaults stood on the corner of High Street and Lad Lane. It was a timber-framed building with a double-gabled

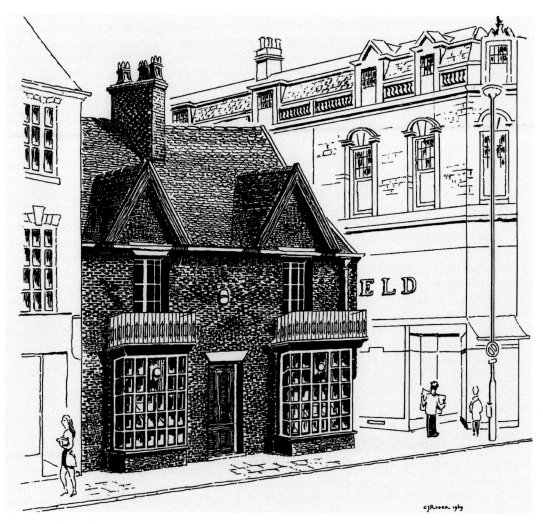

Hind's Vaults, Red Lion Square (drawing, late 1960s).

frontage, later faced with brickwork and given two projecting bay windows surmounted by cast-iron balustrades. The alterations were probably made in 1843, this being the date on the barrel sign that was fixed above the front door. The Globe Commercial Hotel was a florid, brick and terracotta building with a heavily ornamented and shaped central gable that had replaced a hostelry of the same name in 1898. The new hotel was built by Samuel Wilton, whose company was also responsible for the new (Wolstanton School Board) Board Schools in May Bank (1903), Newcastle public baths (1906), Newcastle Sewage Works (1906) and extensions to Enderley Mills. The Central Hotel and neighbouring buildings were replaced by the York Place shopping centre around 1967.

One major change that summed up the new direction in which Newcastle was heading was seen in High Street.

The Castle Hotel opened around 1820 and, although the original building may have been older, the hotel belonged to what might be described as the twilight days of the coaching era in Newcastle. However, by the mid-1960s, the hotel's days were numbered. Trust Houses, who owned the Castle Hotel as well as the Grand Hotel in Hanley, began building the Staffordshire Post House Motor Hotel in May 1966 on the Clayton Road junction with the M6 at Hanchurch. The group's project manager, D. J. Mitchell, announced to the press, 'There was no intention to close the Castle Hotel. The position would be reviewed every year from the point of view of whether the hotel was economic, but he thought there was plenty of business for it to continue.' The new hotel – built on green belt – opened in September 1967, with fifty-three bedrooms and parking space for 118 cars. From the start, it was geared towards motorway users requiring a stopover venue – effectively, the twentieth-century equivalent of the role of the Castle Hotel in the 1820s.

The *Newcastle Times* announced that the hotel was to be demolished in early 1968. On Friday 31 May 1968, manager James Birtlin and his staff staged a farewell party for themselves at the hotel. A sale of the former hotel's furniture and effects took place in the yard and the old ballroom in June 1968, organised by Haywood & Sons, but the building remained intact until 1969 when Tesco Ltd incorporated their new premises into it. This development occurred despite a campaign and a 6,000-name petition to save the Castle Hotel. Ultimately, a decision was made to preserve part of the Georgian facade, with Len Daniels, the secretary of the Newcastle Civic Society, commenting in 1970 that 'It must be understood it was our intention to save the whole hotel but failing this we felt that there was a need to preserve the facade as we felt this was related to the surrounding property and we were afraid the new building would not be in character with the surrounding buildings.'

The Castle Hotel held fond memories for many Newcastilians but, in the following years, other events conspired to disgruntle lovers of traditional pubs in the town.

The hostelry once known as the Star stands in Ironmarket. One of Newcastle's oldest pubs, it is described by the Victoria County History in 1963 as 'a timber-framed building consisting of a two-bay hall parallel with the street, the bays being divided by an open truss with chamfered timbers and an arch-braced tie beam'. It had a deeply rooted community history.

In the 1960s, the pub was extended by Ansells and it was decided to give it a new name with the aim of distinguishing it from all the other pubs called the Star. One of the company's directors, Ted Swain, was a keen gardener, and he suggested the appellation of the Super Star, after a rose which had been cultivated in Germany by distinguished rose breeder Mathius Tantau. The pub was statutorily listed in the early 1970s, but has nevertheless known several changes and alterations, as if the 1960s, in effect, opened the floodgates to a tsunami of mediocrity. In 1983, it was renamed The Boozy Dog and an

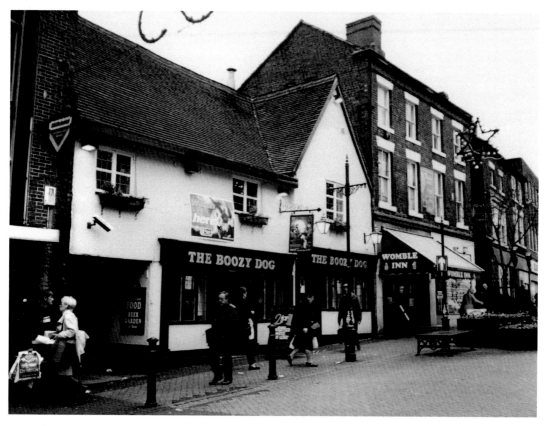

The Boozy Dog, 27 November 2000.

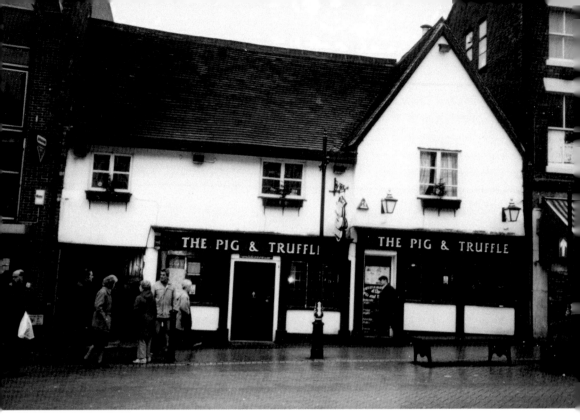

The Pig & Truffle, 19 November 1997.

advertising feature in *The Sentinel* in 1985 referred to the interior having been 'tastefully decorated with thatched, artificial roofs and stuffed animals'. In November 1995, Allied Domecq refurbished and renamed the pub the Pig & Truffle and added a 3-foot-tall hanging sign in the shape of a plastic pig. Borough council leader Eddie Boden criticised the sign for being 'absolutely obnoxious', especially as the pub was in a conservation area. Allied replied that the sign was central to the appeal of the pub and had been approved by the council's planning officers. In 1998, the name of the pub reverted to '(Ye Olde) Boozy Dog' – another attempt to inveigle customers into the pub through the medium of 'plastic heritage'. In February 2003, it became the Reflex 1980s-themed bar.

The pub scene in Newcastle continues to change in accordance with altering tastes and new fads. Truth be told, the town has pursued short-term policies for so many decades now that it seems to be searching desperately for an identity. It is presently undergoing a mini-reinvention as a Real Ale destination, complete with micro-bars – quite a change in direction from the nightclubs and dancing culture of fifteen or twenty years ago. Many pubs of decent vintage survive and their individual histories tell us much about the *Sturm und Drang* of social life in the 'Loyal and Ancient Borough'.

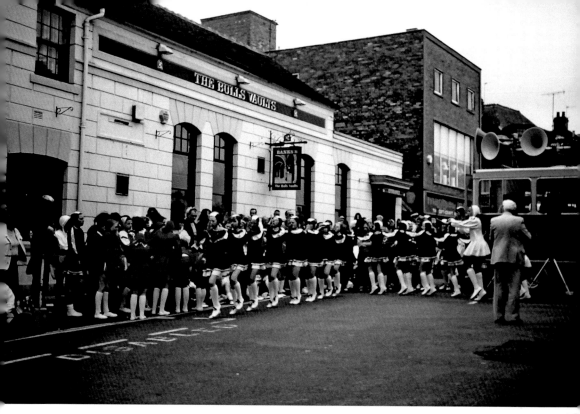

Above: The Bulls Vaults, 26 May 1997 (Newcastle Carnival). This became the Union in December 2009, Lymes in 2011, and the Foyer in August 2014.

Below: The Shakespeare, George Street, 1994.

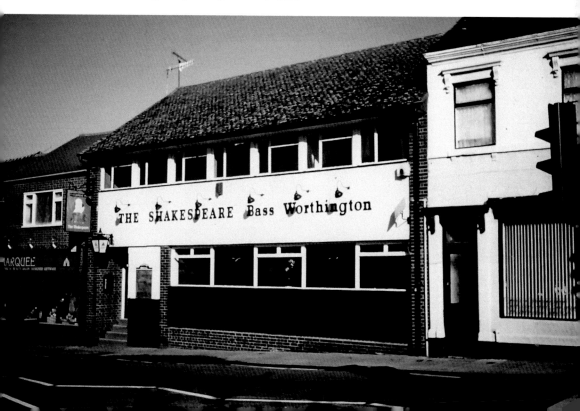

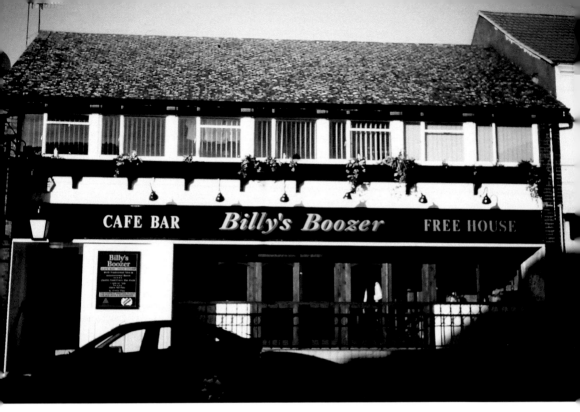

Above: Billy's Boozer, 3 February 1998. The former Shakespeare was renamed Billy's Boozer in 1997, becoming A. J.'s Sports and Entertainment Bar in 2001.

Below: Jolly Potters, Barracks Road, early 1970s.

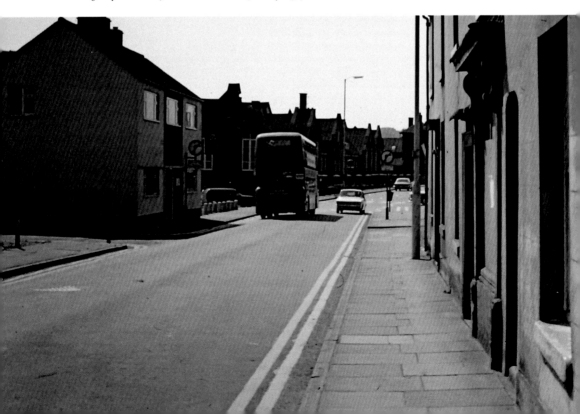

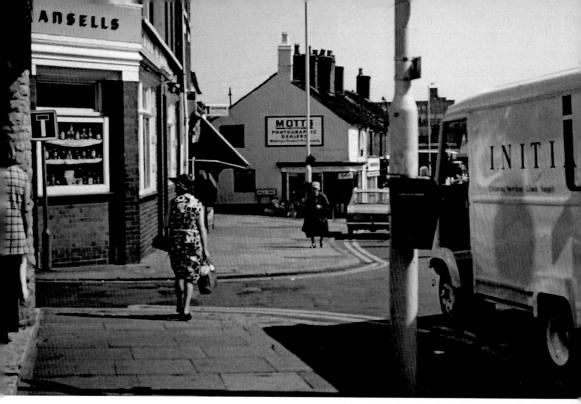

Above: Bird in Hand, Hassell Street, early 1970s.

Right: The Slug and Lettuce, 5 September 1991. The pub became the Fawn and Firkin in June 1994 and has had several names since.

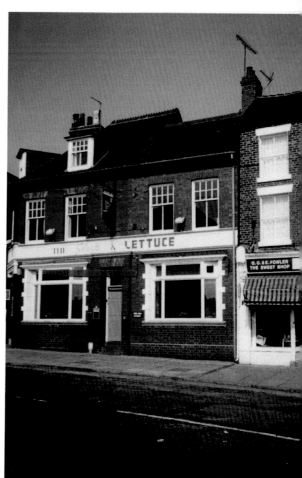

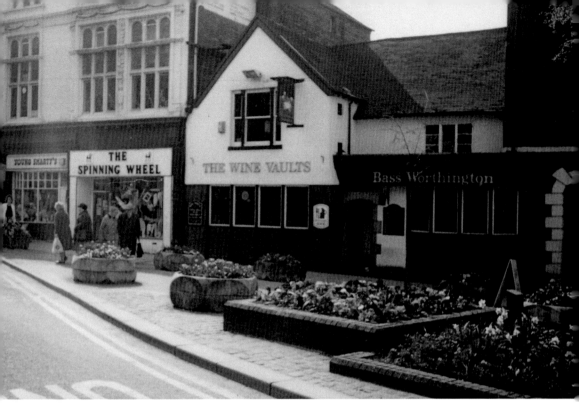

Above: The Wine Vaults, Red Lion Square, April 1990.

Below: The Wine Vaults, 1 July 1994.

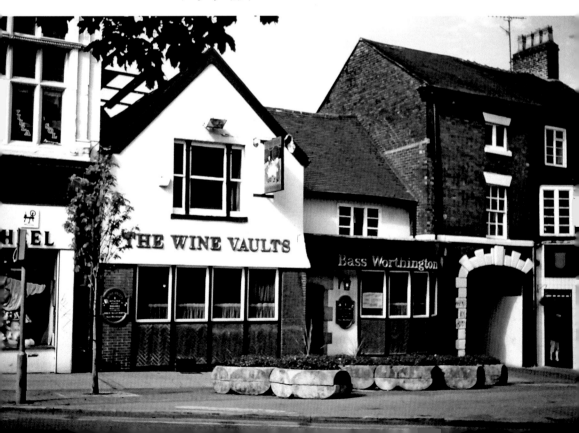

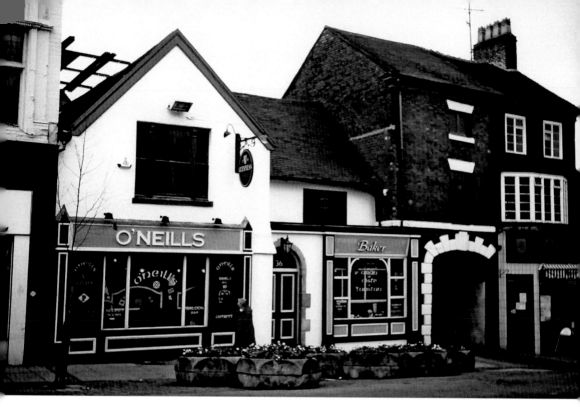

O'Neills, April 1996. The pub became The Wine Vaults again in 2000, On the Square in May 2003, and later the Bedd Bar ('Bedd' standing for 'Bar, eat, drink, dance').

ALBERT, Liverpool Road

The Albert Inn in Liverpool Road opened as a beerhouse in 1861, the year that marked the death of Prince Albert, consort of Queen Victoria. It was advertised as being for sale in May of that year when the household furniture included a mahogany chest of drawers, two corner cupboards, six rush-seated chairs, two oak stands, a round table, a deal leaf table, an eight-day clock in an oak case, another clock in a mahogany case, an armchair, a rocking chair, three feather beds, bolsters and pillows, two sets of bedsteads, two tea trays, saucepans, iron pots, tea kettles and other articles.

In February 1862, landlord William Turner was summoned in connection with a breach of the Beer Act, having been found guilty of allowing two men to drink until 11.40 p.m. Turner was found playing cards with the men, who had a supply of ale on hand. However, relatively few complaints had been made about the running of the beerhouse, and so the bench inflicted a nominal fine of 5s with costs. The beerhouse was advertised as being for sale again in May 1862 when it was said to be attached to a brewhouse, a yard and other buildings. In February 1873, the local press reported on a case of 'the use of obscene and abusive language' by a female customer named Elizabeth Simms who had used provocative words while standing in the entrance to the beerhouse.

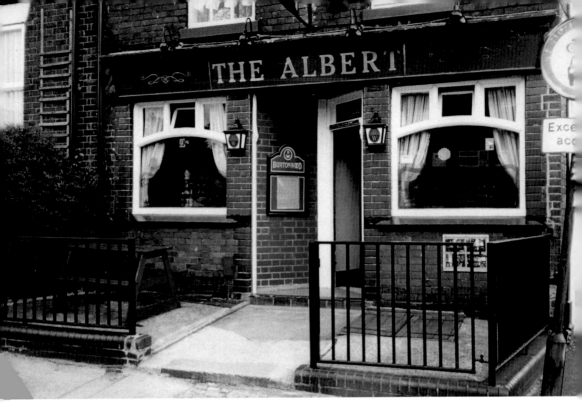

Above: The Albert, 11 July 1998.

Below: The Albert, 13 August 1998.

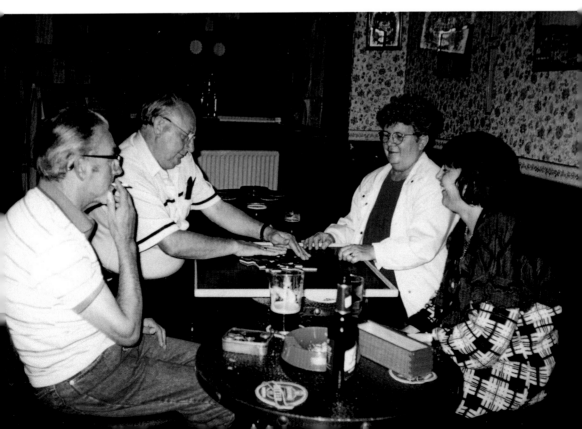

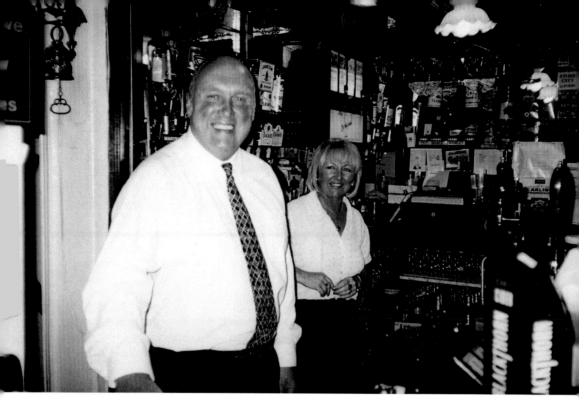

The Albert, with landlord Stan Bennett and wife Sue, 13 August 1998.

At the annual licensing session at Newcastle in 1874, landlord Henry Mansfield applied for a spirit licence, reinforcing his case by telling the justices that he had drawn-up plans for additions and improvements to the premises. However, he was refused. Mansfield applied for a full alehouse licence in 1878, enabling him to sell spirits. Supporting Mansfield was C. Smith (instructed by Mr Griffith) who told the justices that his client had kept the beerhouse for the last sixteen years and that the house was cleanly and well conducted. There was stabling for two horses. It was claimed that there was a customer demand for wines and spirits at the Albert. The brewer, Henry Parker, the owner of the property, testified that he had bought the house for £980 and had spent £554 on improvements. This time, the licence was granted.

In December 1878, there was a gathering of workmen employed at the Cotton Mills in Cross Heath. They met at the Albert to mark the departure from their ranks of James Mayall, who was presented with a silver cruet stand. Mr and Mrs Mansfield laid on a supper for their guests.

George Robinson, aged forty-three, is listed as the licensed victualler in charge of the Albert in the 1881 census, but his tenancy was hardly without incident. In July of that year, he was charged with having been drunk on his own premises and having assaulted police sergeant Swinwood, who had found him 'mad drunk'. The officer had been struck on the ear and knocked to the ground. Robinson, using abusive language, had asked him if he 'wanted any more'. The magistrates fined him £2 in costs, or a month's imprisonment. At this time, the mayor of Newcastle remarked that 'the most disgraceful rows were constantly occurring in Liverpool Road on Saturday nights'. In September, at the adjourned licensing meeting at the Guildhall, Robinson, 'whose licence was withheld in consequence of his being convicted of various offences during the year preceeding the annual licensing meeting, and he not appearing on the occasion to answer to his name being called, now appeared before the Bench'. He was cautioned regarding his future conduct, but his licence was renewed.

Popular landlords in more recent times were Stan and Sue Bennett (pictured), who ran the pub from 1992 until early 2004. Stan, who had an interest in photography, displayed some antique cameras in the pub.

ALBION, High Street

A document in Newcastle Library archives suggests 1832 as the earliest reference to the Albion. A trade directory of 1836 gives James Turner as the licensee of the premises, whose address was No. 20 Penkhull Street. George Gething, the landlord in 1851, also worked as a potter.

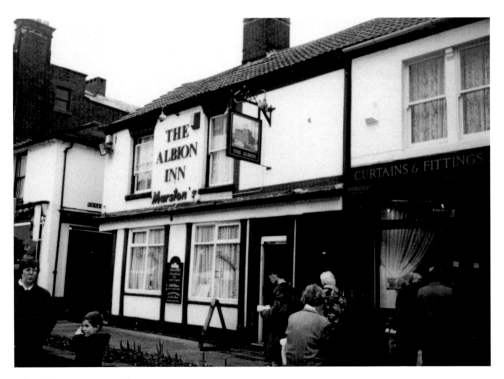

The Albion Inn, 8 February 1993.

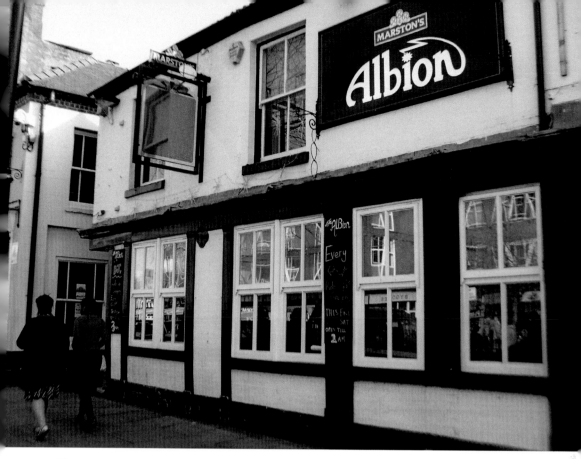

Albion, 1 May 2016.

The Albion's central position in Newcastle made it an attractive venue for meetings. In 1860, a supper was provided for Hulse's Portrait Club, which was 'founded for the purpose of supplying portraits in oil to the members at a small weekly subscription'. The Albion Inn was, at this time, adorned with several finished paintings showcasing the talent of club members. A dinner to the Newcastle fire brigade and several police officers was given in 1864 while in October 1865 a meeting of militant journeymen shoemakers met at the Albion to discuss their grievances over stagnant wages in their trade.

The facilities offered by the Albion are sometimes indicated in the police court reports; for instance, we know that landlord William Hancock was licensed to let out horses for hire – in 1863, he won a court case against a commercial traveller from Birmingham over the loss of a horse and the non-return of a gig and harness. The license of the Albion was transferred from Hancock to Samuel Tate in 1865. Tate (his name sometimes has an alternative spelling in the local newspapers) was fined £1 and costs for selling spirits at illegal hours in 1874. In October of that year, the Albion Inn was put up for sale by auction; the effects included a cart, a pianoforte in a rosewood case, two eight-day clocks, a copper brewing furnace capable of holding 100 gallons and other brewing utensils.

Unfortunately, the unsavoury elements of the town began to associate with the inn in this decade. In 1874, publican Mrs Hannah Broadgate of the Albion Inn appeared before the courts on a charge of permitting prostitutes to remain in the house longer than necessary for refreshment. She had been warned previously. However, there were mitigating circumstances and Hannah was merely cautioned to be careful in the future. Maud Goodwin, described as a 'notorious woman' appeared before the magistrates in 1875 on a charge of being drunk and disorderly and refusing to quit the Albion. She'd only recently been let out of prison, after having served, for the third time in the past year, a term of one month. The court report indicates that she was drunk on arrival at the Albion, but refused to leave, conducting herself in a disorderly manner. She was fined 20s and costs, in default, and served another month in prison. An assault took place at the Albion in 1879 when John Allman, a joiner and builder from Pittshill, pulled Harriet Morris towards him and attempted to take liberties with her. 'She threatened to smash his face, and he then let her go.' He was subsequently fined.

According to CAMRA sources, the Albion Inn almost closed in 1909, on account of 'ladies of ill repute'.

In July 2014, the Albion reopened under new landlord Bill Banks and his wife, Sue Price.

ALMA, George Street

Information gleaned from the archives at Newcastle Library gives 1861 as the likely arrival date of the Alma, whose name recalls the Crimean War battle of 1854. Its address in the early days was sometimes given as Etruria Road. In September 1870, it was stated that the house had been occupied as a beerhouse for eight years.

An early reference to the Alma appears in the local press of 1863, when its landlord was Thomas Hopwood. Thomas Halfpenny was sentenced to one month's imprisonment with hard labour for having stolen a fowl and a brush from Hopwood's premises.

The household furniture of the Alma beerhouse was advertised as for sale in July 1863, the items including brewing vessels, seven barrels, feather beds, straw mattresses, fenders and fire irons.

As a humble beerhouse, the Alma attracted a working-class clientele and occasionally witnessed antisocial behaviour. In 1863, a woman in the street alerted Police Constable Foster of a commotion that was taking place in the Alma. Upon investigation, Foster found a company of men engaged in a fight, but on trying to break it up, he was set upon and abused. Patrick Hart, an

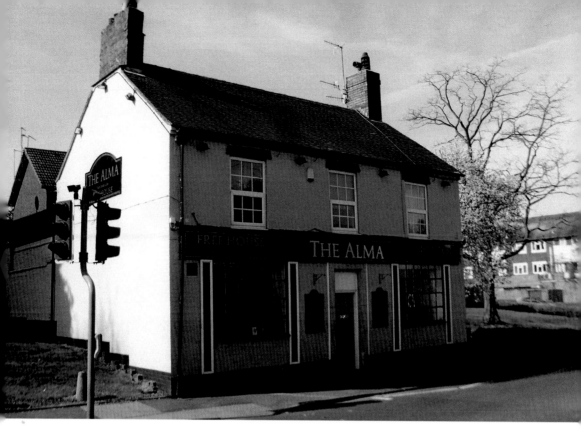

Above: The Alma, 5 May 2016.

Below: The Alma, 6 May 2016.

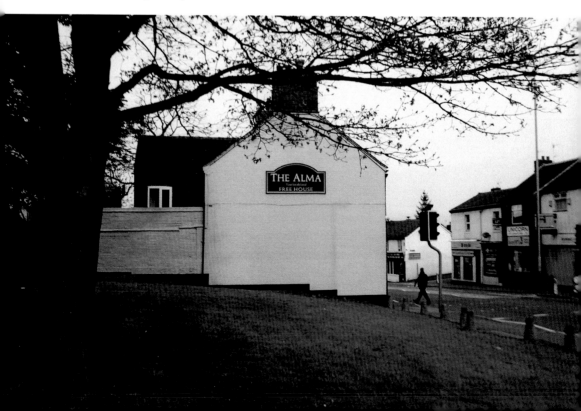

Irishman, seized Foster's staff and hit him with it several times. Hart was later sent to prison for two months with hard labour for his troubles.

John Lowe came to keep the beerhouse. He is certainly mentioned in 1868 as this is when he was accused of permitting card games on the premises. However, the courts exonerated Lowe, 'whose conduct was very creditable to him on the occasion'.

His reputation upheld, Lowe felt confident enough to apply for a spirit licence in 1870. He claimed, through his solicitor, that the Alma was situated near the junction of the Stoke and Hanley Roads, with only one other licensed house in the neighbourhood. The report of this application gives interesting information as to the beginnings of the premises, as it reveals that an application had been made two years previously but refused on the grounds that the Alma was 'not all one house, [but] in reality two houses'. Lowe now felt pleased that he had satisfied the concerns of the licensing magistrates, for he had converted the Alma into one house and had spent over £50 in altering and improving it; it could now boast of several bedrooms and five rooms below. To the rear, there was stabling for three horses and two other stalls could be used if required. His application was granted.

Sadly, Lowe died in May 1872, having decided to ride on his pony and trap to Hanley. The animal bolted and Lowe was thrown to the ground. Bleeding terribly and unconscious, he was driven back to his house, but his life could not be saved.

In 1873, the licence of the Alma was transferred from Mrs Jumps to Ralph Proctor Hand. Soon, he infringed his spirit licence by keeping his house open after 11 p.m., and was subsequently fined 40 shillings and costs, it being decided that 'his licence would have to be endorsed'. Mrs Hand is mentioned as the landlady in June 1875, when she too was summoned for keeping open the beerhouse during prohibited hours. On this occasion, however, the Bench dismissed the case.

In 1877, proprietor George Brown announced on the front page of a local newspaper that the 'Alma Wine and Spirit Vaults' had been stocked with a wide range of beverages and that he had provided a comfortable smoke room and other modern conveniences. These certainly proved attractive to some, as around thirty members of the Hartshill Amateur Christy Minstrels held their annual supper at the Alma in 1880. Coroners' inquests also came to be held on the premises.

An embarrassing transgression was reported in the press in 1885, by which time James Higson, a member of Newcastle Town Council, was the landlord of the Alma. He was fined for keeping the pub open during prohibited hours, though he appears to have been badly let down by his lax manager, Mr Reynolds, and servants. The courts, while having some sympathy with Higson, fined him to the tune of 18s.

The year 1892 saw another interesting case involving the Alma. S. James was an inmate of Stoke Workhouse, along with his wife. It seems that he was formerly a bandmaster with the Northumberland Fusiliers. Going on leave of absence, he had withdrawn £9 in pension and, having deposited £7 in the Post Office Savings Bank, he spent the remainder on drink. He was found drunk and disorderly and refusing to quit the Alma.

The present public house boasts a central bar counter, the Alma's interior having been altered significantly in 1976. Roy Peddle, who had formerly been the tenant of the Oxford Arms in May Bank, and who was then the chairman of the Newcastle Licensed Victuallers' Association, decided to refurbish the pub, spending £10,000 and designing the new interior himself. He converted what had been three small rooms into what was described as a 'spacious one-roomed lounge'. It was further announced that 'It has been tastefully decorated and upholstered to create an atmosphere of the Tudor era, with natural stone fireplaces, oak bar, red draylon-covered seating and original Britannia tables.'

ARNOLD MACHIN, Ironmarket, Newcastle

Here's a story that stands apart from any other in this book – and not just because we are about to feature a venue that is not classed as a 'proper' pub by some drinkers.

Newcastle's former post office was reopened as a pub on 8 July 2002 following an eight-month refurbishment. Its launch in the town was not without controversy and triggered many concerns in respect of what was seen by some as its inappropriate proximity to a local school.

The history of this public house is in its relative infancy, yet it follows the tradition of most J. D. Wetherspoon outlets inasmuch as it doffs its cap to an aspect of local history. What is more, its name has helped to highlight the life and work of a creative talent well worthy of recognition.

Ceramic artist Arnold Machin, OBE, RA, was born into a family of pottery workers at Oakhill in 1911 and attended Burslem School of Art. He became a Royal Academician, with his work produced by Minton and Wedgwood in addition to Royal Worcester and Crown Derby.

He refused to join the armed forces in the Second World War, as a conscientious objector. He was subsequently sentenced to a year in Wormwood Scrubs – notwithstanding letters of support from Josiah Wedgwood and P. H. Jowett, the Principal of the Royal College of Art – and was incarcerated with murderers and rapists. Fortunately, he was released after nine months, before being employed as a full-time figure modeller at Wedgwood's.

In 1942, he modelled bas relief portraits of Churchill and Roosevelt for use on embossed Queensware mugs. They were emblazoned with the words, 'Give us the tools and we will finish the job,' and 'It can be done, it will be done,

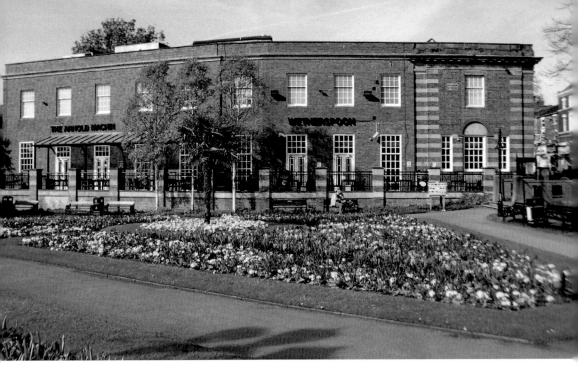

Above: The Arnold Machin, from Queen Elizabeth Gardens, 5 May 2016.

Below: The Arnold Machin, 15 October 2012.

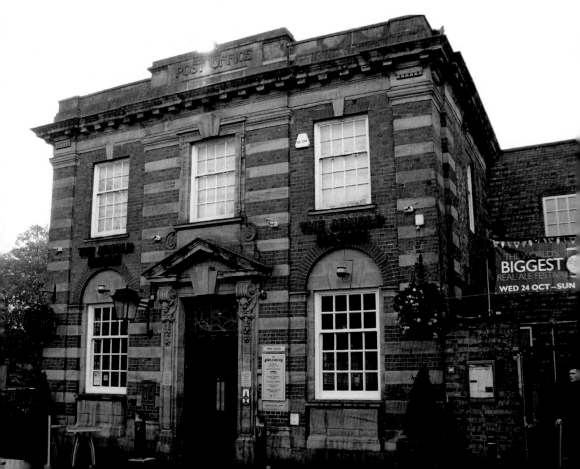

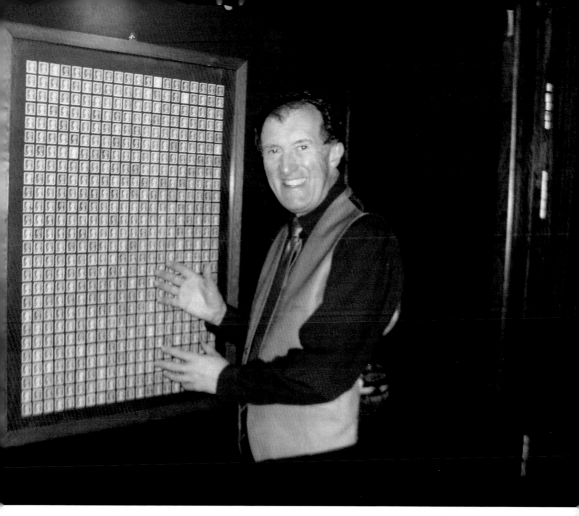

The Arnold Machin interior, with Mervyn Edwards indicating the stamp display.

it must be done.' Following the war, Machin modelled black basalt busts of Elizabeth II and the Duke of Edinburgh.

Some of his work came to be bought by the Tate Gallery and, in 1947, he was elected an Associate of the Royal Academy of Arts.

In 1956, Machin chained himself to a Victorian gas lamppost at The Villas in Stoke in defiance of the seven workmen who had come to uproot it. It was scheduled to be replaced by a concrete electric lamp standard. Machin was reported to have said, 'This is my protest against the destruction of beautiful things which is going on in this country.' Machin and his wife Pat attached themselves to their beloved lamp post for six and a half hours, using an umbrella to shield themselves from the blazing sunshine, before the police were called.

However, Machin is probably best known for having designed the Queen's portrait for the definitive postage stamps that first appeared in 1967. This became the most reproduced image in history.

Machin, who died in 1999, would have had much to say about the area immediately around the pub that bears his name. The adjacent Queen's Gardens is one of the most beautiful pockets of Newcastle and we should remember that he found gardens a source of inspiration and calm. However, the man who decried 'the stupidity of the modern subtopian age' may have disapproved of the demolition of the Victorian former St Giles and St George's School to the rear of the gardens, which was taken down in April 2016 in order to make way for a modern 'council hub'.

In 2007, the memoirs of Machin, entitled *Artist of an Icon* and edited by Barbara Went, were published by Frontier. In the same year, a commemorative miniature sheet of stamps bearing Arnold Machin's face was released. He is remembered as a quiet man and a gentleman.

My first visit to the Arnold Machin pub was on 8 July 2002 and I recorded the following in my pub log:

> Before the Potteries Pub Preservation Group and other interested parties began kicking up a fuss, this was to have been a Lloyds Number One outlet. These hostelries are essentially the trendier siblings of the mainstream Wetherspoon's pubs. The eleventh-hour change of heart on the part of the company certainly shows. The Arnold Machin is neither traditional in atmosphere, nor up-to-the-minute trendy. It falls between two stools, and may even prosper as a result of this ambiguous appeal. There are collections of postage stamps exhibited in frames and interpretation explaining the contribution of Arnold Machin, whose likeness of the Queen has appeared on stamps since 1967.

BLACK FRIAR, High Street

The pub was originally known as the Spread Eagle. Information in Newcastle Library archives traces it back to 1832 at the latest. The hostelry is not mentioned among the fifty-three pubs listed in the 1822–23 trade directory, but a directory for 1836 gives the address of the Spread Eagle as No. 70 Penkhull Street. It was then kept by James Worrall and was listed under retailers of beer, rather than taverns and public houses. By 1851, it was kept by G. Foote, and certainly by 1860 by J. Woodhouse. In that year, *Kelly's Directory* lists a George Lakin operating as a dealer in tobacco and pipe clay, based in nearby Paradise Street. This is likely to be the George Lakin who is mentioned in the police court reports of 1864 as the landlord of the Spread Eagle. He was fined for selling beer during prohibited hours. Lakin appeared before the courts again in 1870 in connection with alleged gambling on the premises on Whit Monday. The judges looked sympathetically on his case, believing him not to have encouraged the gambling of the men involved, but this mention in the

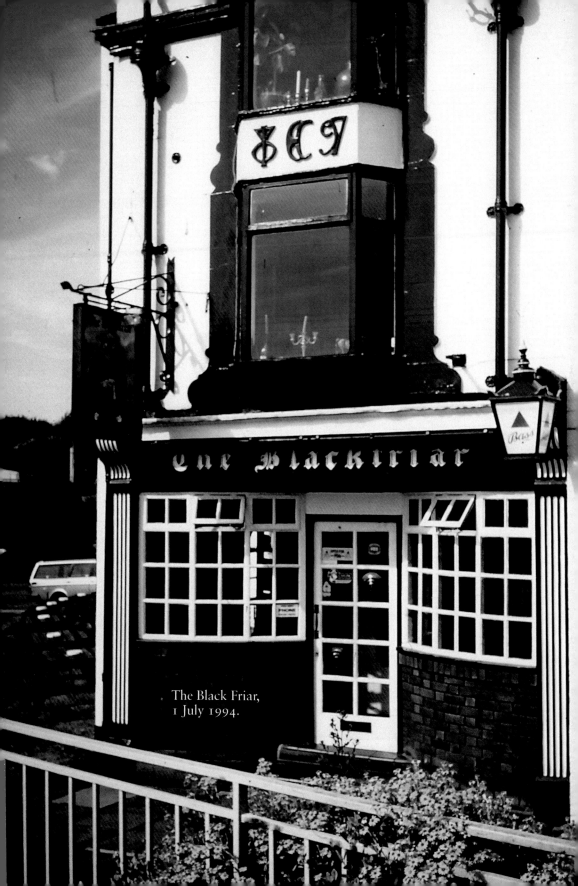

The Black Friar,
1 July 1994.

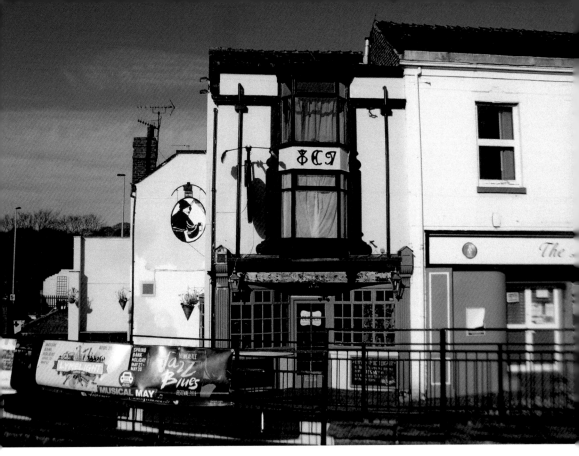

The Black Friar, 3 May 2016.

press is interesting because it informs us that the Spread Eagle had a skittle alley at the time, hence the alleged betting.

In February 1876, the Spread Eagle, incorporating a large yard to the rear, was advertised as for sale by auction, still under the occupation of Lakin. The property was then adjoined by a hairdressers and several other properties, also offered as lots. However, we know that Lakin was still the landlord in 1882, as he was brought before the magistrates' courts having allegedly been drunk and abusive on his own premises. Lakin was fined a small sum by an evidently disinterested court, his transgression apparently having taken place after closing time.

The previously noted auction mentions the contiguous properties that will only be remembered now by those born before the 1960s. These buildings stretched all the way down to where Penkhull Street joined Goose Street and Stubbs Gate. The major upheaval in Newcastle in the 1960s incorporated the building of the new A34 ring road and the Grosvenor 'sunken' roundabout, all of which was to ease traffic congestion in the town. Surviving photographs show the Spread Eagle neatly tucked in among a row of premises, with George

Hollins & Son on its immediate right. All properties to the left of the pub were demolished as part of the restructuring of this part of the town.

The name change to the Black Friar in 1977 recognised the close proximity of the site to the medieval friary of Blackfriars. This jettisoning of its traditional name in order to promote a little plastic heritage subsequently led to the pub being known rather frivolously by some as the Dirty Vicar. However, a far worse fate was to afflict the long-established Newcastle hostelry in 1995. In November of that year, it became one of a number of pubs across the country to embrace the vogue for bogus Irishness. The Black Friar reopened, advertising itself as Newcastle's first Irish bar, promoting traditional Irish music, traditional Irish food and drinks such as Guinness, Murphys and Beamish. Other Newcastle hostelries – notably the Old Bull's Head in Lad Lane – also became Irish-themed pubs, prompting the Black Friar's landlord, John Light, to tell *The Sentinel* newspaper, 'We were the first to open as an Irish pub – now the big breweries are jumping on the bandwagon. There will be too many in the town soon.' Thankfully, no ersatz Irish pubs survive in town today, and the Black Friar offers quizzes and traditional pub entertainment.

BOROUGH ARMS HOTEL, King Street

A pottery works in Newcastle was established by James Bulkeley and William Bent in 1790 or 1791. They built what is now the old part of the Borough Arms Hotel, on the corner of Water Street, as part of their pottery manufactory. The unsuccessful business was dissolved in November 1797.

However, Bent (the driving force behind the original failed partnership) converted the pot-bank into a brewery, a pottery oven becoming a malt kiln in the process. His new business partners were James Caldwell, a potter, and James Barrow, a local financier. According to the historian W. J. Thompson, Bent's brewery was based in Newcastle between 1799 and 1836, in which year it moved to Liverpool. The premises were then transferred to Messrs Rogers, Hindle and Baker of the North Staffordshire Brewery in Water Street, which became Baker & King (1867) and King's Brewery in 1886.

The opening of a railway passenger station in King Street in 1852, serving travellers between Stoke, Newcastle and Silverdale, was a major factor in the decision to apply for a licence in 1853 to convert part of the brewery site into an inn. The Borough Arms opened shortly after.

In 1861, there is a report of disorder at the hotel between two cattle dealers from Longton, who were fined by the local magistrates for their disorderly behaviour.

The 1861 census records the Borough Arms in Upper King Street being kept by Mary Webb (an unmarried sixty-two-year-old hotelkeeper) living with a son, two daughters and two servants. The Webb family history, researched

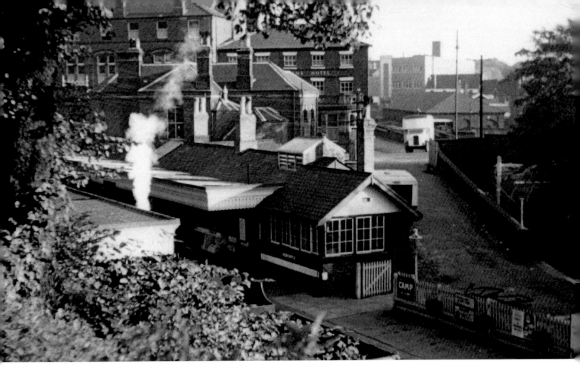

Above: Borough Arms and adjacent railway station, early 1960s.

Below: Borough Arms, 5 May 2016.

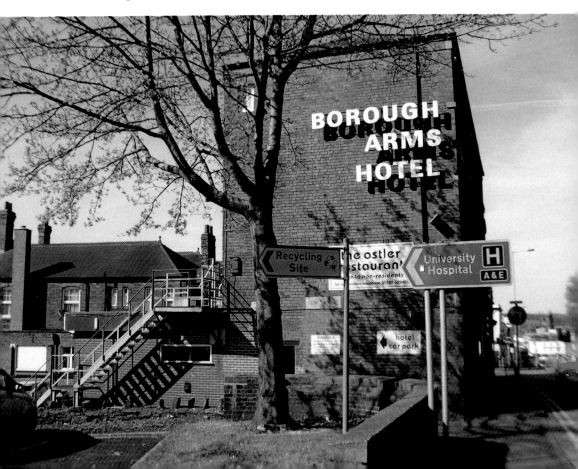

by genealogist Mervyn Selleck, indicates however that Mary Webb was not 'unmarried' as she had married Edward James Webb in 1820. Mr Selleck adds that Edward died through 'decay of nature', on 11 October 1855 aged fifty-nine, so Mary would have been a widow. The death of 'Edward Webb, landlord of the Borough Arms' is recorded in at least two local newspapers with the *Newcastle Journal* giving his age as fifty-eight.

Mr Selleck's research shows that Mary Webb's daughter, Mary Anne Webb, married Samuel Hyslop on 3 February 1864.

The year 1869 was to prove a significant year in the story of the Borough Arms Hotel. It was announced in the press that Samuel Hyslop had taken the hotel, 'conducted by miss webb, and family for the last fifteen years'. Mr Selleck records that this Miss Webb was probably Catherine Webb. Rather inauspiciously, Hyslop was attacked in 1869 by a drunken cook, Mary Marshall, in that year. 'She broke two banisters, bit the complainant through the arm, and kicked him until he was quite black. She went into the kitchen, and taking a saucepan from the fire, threw it at Mr Hyslop. Her conduct was very violent.' She was sent to prison for a month.

The Borough Arms was well-equipped to provided food for various gatherings from the 1860s onwards. Following a local Volunteers' drill on Wolstanton Marsh in 1861, the men afterwards proceeded to the Borough Arms for refreshments. Events held in Stubbs Walks, such as the Newcastle Horticultural and Allotment Society's exhibitions, boasted refreshment tents – Mr Hyslop being the caterer in August 1870.

Storms and severe flooding of local streets, houses and pubs occurred in August 1872. Upper King Street was just one of the thoroughfares affected by the floodwater: 'The stream rushed into the yard of the Borough Arms Hotel, literally swimming the pigs out of the stys, flooding the stables, and rushing into the cellars of the brewery of Mr. C. H. King. Here, great damage and heavy loss must result.

By this time, it was becoming clear that the popularity of the Borough Arms (especially among the middle classes and the societies to which they belonged) was beginning to necessitate an extension to the premises. The proximity of the railway station remained a source of revenue to Hyslop, while the Newcastle Theatre at the foot of Brunswick Street also benefited the hotel. In 1872, Hyslop applied to the magistrates to grant him an extension beyond the hour of 11 p.m. on the nights the theatre was open. He argued that 'each night traps had to be put up at his stables, and they had to be got after the house was closed, and the owners wanting refreshments could not have it'. In January 1873, the magistrates permitted Hyslop to keep the hotel open until midnight in order to accommodate the supper of post office officials.

By this time, Hyslop's status in the town of Newcastle had been elevated through his commercial interests and his high profile as a civic dignitary. Information contained within a *Graphic Description of Newcastle-under-Lyme 1893* in Newcastle Reference Library tells us that he was born in Dumfries in May 1830 (although the 1871 Census records his age in that year as being only thirty-nine), and commenced his career as a draper in 1848. He began trading in Newcastle in 1858 and had married Mary Ann Webb, the fourth daughter of the late Mr Edward Webb, in 1864. He became a member of the town council in 1868 and was mayor between 1872 and 1873. In April 1874, a 'dinner and presentation to the ex-mayor of Newcastle' took place at the Borough Arms in his honour.

In November 1874, the Borough Arms was offered for sale by auction at the North Stafford Hotel, Stoke, with Hyslop the occupier, and Mr Johnson, of the Tunstall Brewery, having the bidding to themselves. Hyslop was ultimately able to purchase it for £3,360.

Hyslop, now being the owner of the hotel, was more able to bring some of his major plans to fruition. In 1876, at the annual meeting of the North Staffordshire Licensed Victuallers Society, Hyslop, as president, had argued that 'with regard to the enlargement of property he said he thought the magistrates would see the inconsistency of preventing an enlargement of premises where it was required to meet the public convenience'. A new assembly room was subsequently built to further accommodate social gatherings. It was erected in February 1878 and fronted King Street: 'The basement is used as a refreshment room and billiard room, the latter being supplied with a new table by Orme & Sons of Manchester. The assembly room fills – with the exception of the space occupied by the staircase – the entire dimensions of the first floor. It is forty-five feet in length by twenty-two feet in width; it is well-ventilated, and is lighted by five large windows at the front and two at the back. Ample space is offered in the room for dining 150 persons. Over the assembly room there are six bedrooms. The whole of the new building is heated with hot air.'

The public dinner that accompanied the opening was attended by seventy-plus guests, Alderman Mellard (the mayor of Newcastle) presiding, and Alderman Miller and Mr C. H. King occupying the vice chairs. Mellard 'remembered the Borough Arms before it was a licensed house, and he also remembered the father and mother of the present hostess keeping the house when it was first licensed. It had continued with the family ever since; and though the family name of the proprietor was changed, there was still to be seen the excellence of the old family management. From one member of the family to another the business had passed until it came into the hands of the present host, a gentleman who, like others of his nationality who had settled in this town, had not made bad use of his time since he came to the borough. He was sure it was a happy day for Mr. Hyslop when he met the present hostess'. Hyslop, responding, said that he 'had long contemplated an enlargement of the hotel, but was unable to make a satisfactory arrangement with the then owner. A few years ago, however, he became the purchaser of the premises; and thought the provision of additional accommodation had been delayed for a time, it was now an accomplished fact. It was no ambitious motive which had prompted the enlargement of his house. Its contiguity to the railway station caused it to be frequented by large numbers of persons, and the amount of commercial business which came to the house rendered additional accommodation necessary. Then there were frequently meetings and large sales held at the house, for which the rooms in the old building were scarcely suitable'.

Hyslop advertised the new, improved hotel in the local press as suitable for (among others) commercial travellers and families: 'The New Wing contains a large number of Bedrooms, all Newly Furnished; also Commercial, Coffee and Billiard Rooms, with extensive Stock Rooms, and a large Assembly Room for Dinners, Public Meetings, Sales, & c.'

The new accommodation was swiftly brought into requisition, and, in 1878, the annual dinners of Hartshill Football Club and Hartshill Cricket Club were both held at the hotel. There was also a dinner for the employees of the North Staffordshire Brewery, organised by Mr C. H. King, on the occasion of his son Charles King's marriage. In 1879, the North Staffordshire Curling Club, which was based at the nearby rink, met at the hotel for their annual dinner – as they would do in future years. The rink itself also played host to Rose Shows and Hyslop acted as caterer on these occasions. Hyslop suffered minor embarrassment in August 1879 when, at the annual licensing meeting for the Borough, he (as chairman of the LVA) was accused of never having applied to the magistrates 'for an extension of his licence to the large new premises which he had added to the Borough Arms, and in which he was in the habit of selling drink'. His licence was temporarily withheld, but renewed without much opposition at a special court held in September.

Hyslop became Mayor of Newcastle again in 1892–93. He is listed as proprietor of the hotel in the 1900 *Kelly's Directory*, but died in 1901.

In 1916, the proprietors of the hotel served notice in the press that they were giving up the posting business. Among the items they advertised for sale were broughams, landaus, dog carts and gigs.

CASTLE MONA, Victoria Street, Newcastle

Numerous public houses first operated as humble beerhouses, often run by enterprising individuals carrying on a secondary trade, reducing the chances of insolvency. In 1862, James Hall, a cutler by profession, placed a notice in the local press that he had removed from High Street and was now based

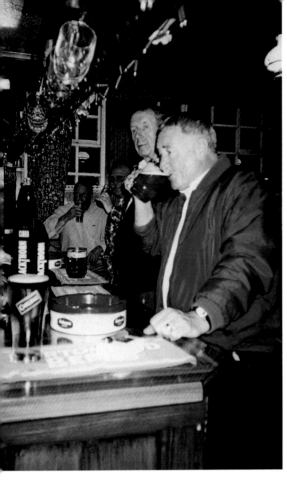

Left: Castle Mona, 13 August 1998.

Below: Castle Mona, 2 October 2000.

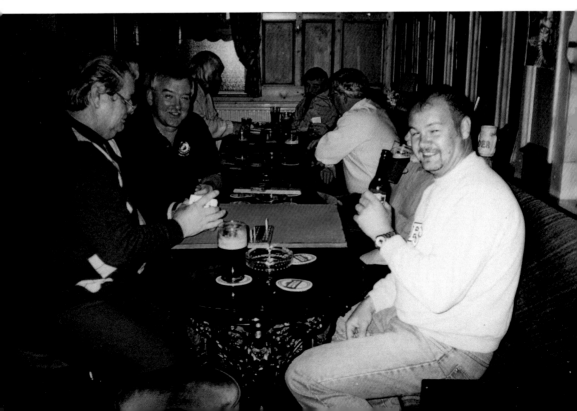

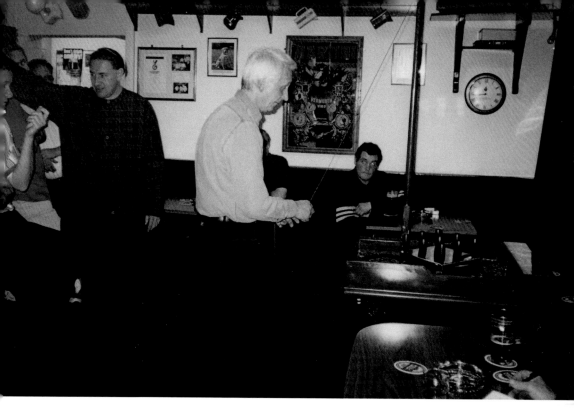

Above: Castle Mona, bar room, 2 October 2000.

Below: Castle Mona, 7 August 2013.

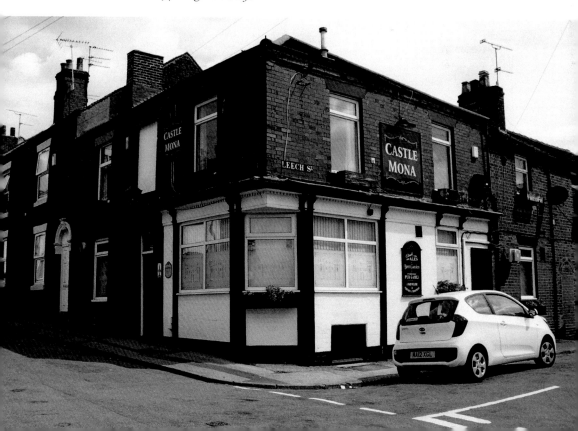

at the Castle Mona in London Road. The premises at this time were often given the address of London Road, presumably to more easily identify their location.

The Castle Mona beerhouse was advertised as being up for sale by auction in September 1863. The furniture at this time included 'a handsome 8-day clock in oak case, chest of drawers, four-post and tent bedsteads, feather and flock beds, straw mattress and bedding, round and square deal table, chimney and dressing glasses, time piece, fender and fire irons, brass candlesticks, bird and cage, cooking and kitchen utensils, and other effects. Also sign and name board, drinking screens and brass taps'. Shop fixtures, stock-in-trade and the premises' working plant, which included a small steam engine and boiler, an anvil, a vice and other tools, remind us that Mr Hall was first and foremost a tradesman by profession.

By November, Mr Hall gave notice of his removal from the Castle Mona to premises at the top of High Street, next door to Mr Franck, an optician.

The Castle Mona, fresh on the market, was subsequently advertised in the press as a desirable business opportunity in December:

> The premises contain front shop with plate glass window, parlour, bar, and bar parlour, tap-room, scullery with iron pump and a plentiful supply of water, cellar, good yard, and cutler's shop, which may be readily converted into a butcher's shop or a workshop for an artificer. There are also two good bedrooms, and clothes closet, and large club-room. The house is fitted up with good grates, iron washing furnace, and gas, and is well adapted for any business, requiring space, is situated in a respectable neighbourhood, where a good class of houses are constantly in course of erection.

The same notice appeared in the press in March 1864, and the Castle Mona was ultimately taken on by William Audley. He had been listed in *Kelly's Trade Directory* (1860) as an auctioneer, appraiser, house and estate agent, with offices at Pepper Street in Newcastle as well as at Stone and Hanley. William Audley lost no time in announcing his arrival as Mr Hall's successor at the Castle Mona, advertising his 'First-class ales, porter, and cider, cigars, tobacco, and good accommodation' in a local newspaper. Unfortunately, he fell foul of the sessions of the Borough petty sessions in 1865, having to plead guilty to the charge of having his house open for the sale of beer during prohibited hours on a Sunday. He was duly fined.

In September 1868, it was announced that Mr J. Pilsbury had been granted a licence at the Castle Mona. John Pilsbury, born in Newcastle, was keeping the Castle Mona at the time of the 1871 census when he was listed as a butcher and an innkeeper. Sarah Leigh is mentioned in the census, listed as a 'butcher's apprentice'. John, 'Castle Mona, & butcher', was listed in *Kelly's Trade Directory* of 1872, but by August of that year, the household furniture, butcher's utensils and stock-in-hand on the premises were up for sale, the press advertisement being pitched at 'butchers, publicans and others'. Items included a spring cart, butcher's block, scales and weights and a cleaver.

By 1880, the beerhouse was occupied by the Meadon family and they are recorded as being in residence in the 1881 census. By the time of the 1891 census, Edward Starkey and his family kept the Castle Mona. He is listed, rather loftily, as a brewer's manager, while a trade directory of 1892 describes him as a publican.

Reminiscences about the pub's twentieth-century history, courtesy of George Goode who was born in Victoria Street in 1916 and who became a regular at the pub, can be found in my book, *Great Pubs Around Stoke-on-Trent* (Churnet Valley Books, 2001).

CRICKETERS ARMS, Alexandra Road, May Bank

The Cricketers' Arms overlooks Wolstanton Marsh and was originally a small beerhouse opened to cater for the sportsmen and spectators who gathered on the marsh. From the early nineteenth century, foot-racing, pugilistic bouts, rabbit-coursing and cricket (played by such teams as Wolstanton Victoria, Newcastle-under-Lyme Star and Freehold Villa of Burslem) were popular attractions on the marsh.

The beerhouse appears to have opened in the 1830s and, by 1857, it was certainly known by the name of the Cricketers' Arms. In this year, it was advertised as being up for sale by auction, being in the occupation of Adam Hodgkins, beerseller. It contained eight rooms and a capacious club room which could accommodate 100 people. Outbuildings included a brewhouse and stabling for two horses, and there was also a skittle ground and a garden. The owner at the time was William Barker. The auction particulars reveal that the beerhouse had been recently improved at some cost, indicating that it was trading well through the crowds who watched the local sport and who found themselves in need of refreshment. The establishment was again advertised to be sold by private contract in 1859, with Mr Barker stating in his notice that the premises were 'well adapted for a butcher, or any other business requiring considerable room'. The Cricketers' Arms was similarly up for auction in 1863 – particulars referred to a 'newly-erected barn' attached to the premises.

In 1880, there was a sale of useful household furniture and blacksmith's tools at the Cricketers' Arms on account of the anticipated departure of beerseller Samuel Birks. Among the items up for sale were four hair-seated chairs, mahogany bedsteads, a barometer, patent bellows, crowbars and hammers. Birks is listed in some of the trade directories as a blacksmith and a beerseller,

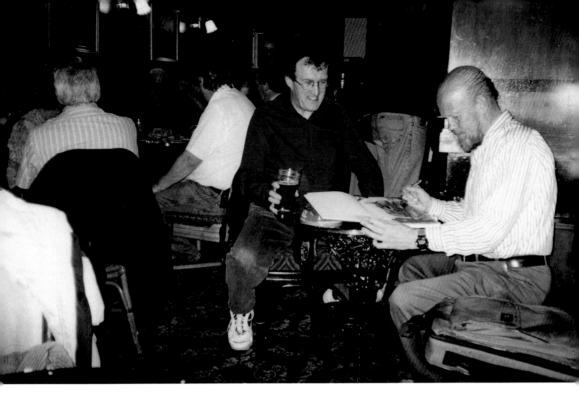

Above: Cricketers Arms, 4 October 2000. Mervyn Edwards with the late David Gregory, artist (d. 2004).

Below: Cricketers Arms in snow, 26 December 2004.

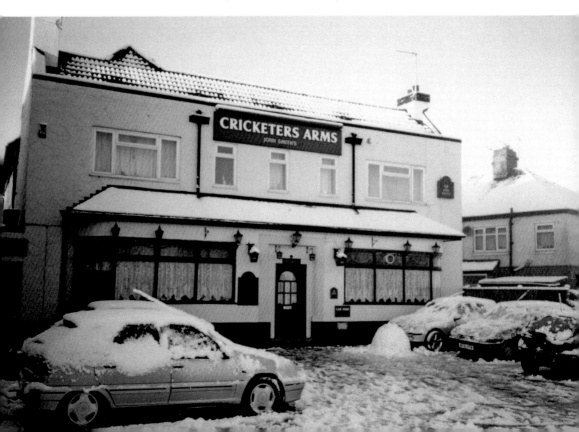

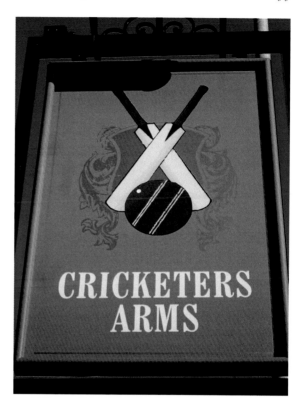

Cricketers Arms sign, 15 April 2015.

illustrating the sometimes precarious status of a beerseller and the need to have a second means of income.

Evidence that the beerhouse was looking to expand is seen in the application of its licensee, Thomas Maiden, for a beer and wine licence, in August 1887. However, the application was refused at that time.

A photograph from *c.* 1933, available in Newcastle Borough Museum and Art Gallery, shows the pub shortly before being rebuilt. At this stage, it was tied to Parker's Burslem Brewery; and a courtyard in front was enclosed by a brick wall.

Plans for alterations at the Cricketers Arms were submitted to Newcastle Borough Council in August 1936.

Darts legend Phil Taylor became the landlord in 1993. The pub underwent a refurbishment, costing £80,000, in 2014. The current (2016) landlord is Steve Dawe and the present building is finished in trowel-effect rendering.

CROWN, Brook Street, Silverdale

The only two Silverdale pubs listed in *White's Directory* (1851) are the Bush, kept by John Kent, victualler, and the Sneyd's Arms, kept by Adam Mountford, maltster and victualler. So what appears to be an early reference to the Crown appears in September 1856, when the local press referred to the fact that

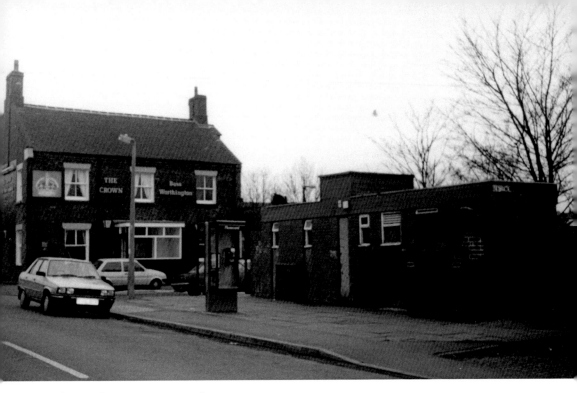

Above: The Crown, 2 March 1993.

Below: Crown Inn, 2 February 2016.

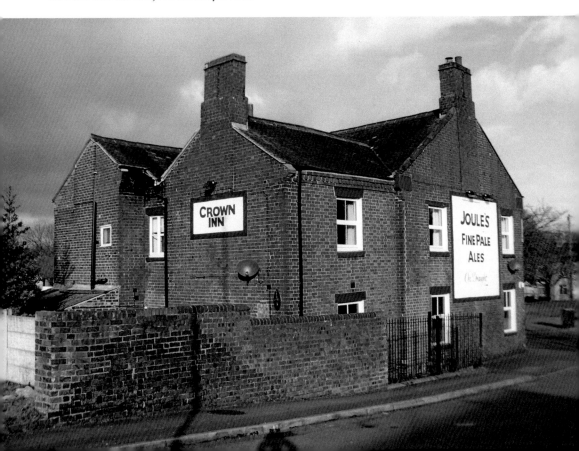

George Oldfield had applied for the transfer of the licence from the Sneyd's Crest at Scot Hay to the Crown Inn at Silverdale – it was granted.

The Crown was associated for many years with the Oddfellows Friendly Society, and a report in the local press in 1856 is a typical description of an anniversary celebration. The Good Samaritan Lodge of the Manchester Unity of Odd Fellows and their friends – around 160 in number – met at the Crown and processed to St Luke's Church, where a sermon was preached by the Revd G. Armitage. Afterwards they walked through the village accompanied by a musical band, before returning to the Crown Inn, where a tent had been erected for their accommodation. Dinner was provided for them by landlord Mr G. Oldfield.

The Crown and the adjacent area was also a popular meeting place for Silverdale miners. Several members of the North Staffordshire Miners' Association held an open-air meeting near the Crown Inn in 1863.

Michael Brown had kept the Crown from early 1861, but three years later he moved to the Bush Inn, and the Crown's licence was transferred to Charles Noden (sometimes spelt as Nodin).

The pub hosted many auctions of local land and property. In 1863, a beerhouse in Mill Street, known as the Plough, was auctioned at the Crown. A tailor's and clothier's shop, fronting Victoria Street and Crown Street, was sold at the Crown in 1893.

Coroners' inquests took place at the Crown, and these were described in the local newspapers; for example, in 1865 Daniel Rushton, manager of the Knutton Forge, suffered a fatal injury at work when the handle of a crane slipped out of a colleague's hands and struck him on the head and killing him. In the same year, another inquest took place at the Crown in respect of a Newcastle woman who had dropped dead after lifting a bucket of potatoes into her cart in a field at Finney Green. One man, a collier from Audley, died after a drinking spree, being 'a man of drunken habits'. The inquest was convened at the Crown in 1869.

The proprietors of the Mill Bank Colliery held a supper to its workers there in 1866 with around 150 present. Each man was given a quart of ale and there was much jollity, with music from the New Connexion Singers and a recitation of the Barrel Organ by Mr H. Harvey, inducing much laughter. Mr Noden appears to have been a popular food caterer, for he provided food at a grand gala in connection with Wolstanton Wakes, held in a field near the Sneyd Arms, in 1874. He even set up the Crown Inn soup kitchen in 1879, catering for many weeks for the poor people of Silverdale. One week in February of that year saw 643 quarts of soup and 228 loaves being given to the impoverished.

The Noden family's involvement in the licensed trade would have exposed them to the misbehaviour of many well-known rogues. There were few in

Silverdale more incorrigible than Benjamin Hollins, a collier, who appeared before the courts on numerous occasions for drunkenness. In 1881, Sarah Noden – daughter of the landlord – told the courts that the drunk and disorderly Hollins had been asked to leave the Crown, but had declined to do so. He was offered 2d as an incentive to leave, but had to be forcibly ejected. Outside the Crown, he kicked police constable Critchlow and struck him in the stomach. He was sentenced to a month's hard labour.

The Crown hosted entertainments for soldiers, courtesy of the Silverdale Welcome Home Committee, in March 1919. A total of 143 First World War returned soldiers were honoured at the Crown with a dinner and gifts of beer and tobacco.

One senior citizen who knew the Crown well talked to the local press in 1973. Florence Barker, of Abbey Street, came from a family who had run a news agency business in Silverdale. However, she had been born in the pub, which had been kept by her father, and remembered that he brewed his own beer, fetching water from a water spout in Back Lane. She also recalled the pub's bowling green.

A memorable landlord at both the Vine and the Crown in Silverdale was Don Waghorn. In 1990, it was reported that he and his wife Barbara were keeping a six-month-old Vietnamese pot-bellied pig in a sty in the Vine's backyard. They named it Worthington, though it drank milk rather than ale. In 1992, the Waghorns moved to the Crown, taking their pig with them. *The Evening Sentinel* recorded that Worthington saw a double bed, the property of the Crown's outgoing landlord, Eddie Roberts, in the pub's yard, and had started eating its wooden and cloth base. Eddie, who moved to the Travellers Rest at Milton, told the newspaper, 'He ripped some of the cloth and chewed the wood but luckily he was caught before he did any more damage. You've got to see the funny side of it.'

In 2014, the Potteries branch of CAMRA reported in its magazine *Potters Bar* that the Crown Inn in Silverdale was 'thriving under its Joules ownership'.

CROWN, Talke Road, Red Street, Chesterton

The Crown is listed in an 1818 trade directory as being kept by Isaac Emberton. In 1832, Henshall Moss was stated as running the inn at the time of a sale by auction of local land that embraced the Roebuck Inn in Chesterton. *Pigot's Directory* of 1835 lists Richard Moss as keeping the Crown, and in 1837 another auction took place there, to wit the sale of 'a new messuage or dwelling house … called the King's Arms, situate at Red Street'.

Brief mention should be made of the importance of the Moss family. They were the last in Red Street to make crockery, but gave this up *c.* 1845 in the interests of brick and tile, which they had been making since the eighteenth

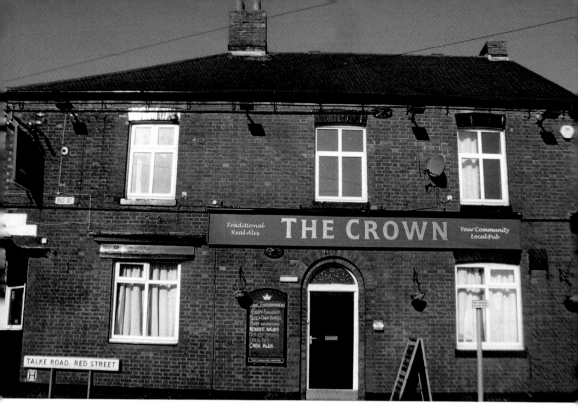

Above: The Crown, 5 May 2016.

Below: The Crown, 5 May 2016.

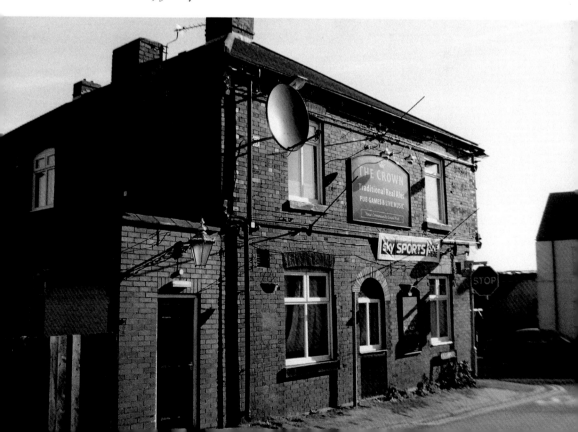

century. Thomas and Henshall Moss appear in a list of manufacturers of earthenware, bricks and tile in 1796. Henshall Moss kept another Red Street pub, the Wheatsheaf, but died aged seventy-eight in 1833. Richard Moss also made earthenware and Egyptian black at Red Street in addition to keeping the Crown. He died in 1847, aged sixty-four.

George Woolliscroft, a builder, was the innkeeper by 1851, but in July 1863, the Crown, described as 'a roadside house, and doing excellent business', was up for sale – 'rent moderate'.

The coroner's inquests that took place at the Crown allow us a view of life in Red Street in the nineteenth century. In 1877, Thomas William Dean, aged four, was one of three children left at home while his mother took her husband's breakfast to a neighbouring colliery. In her absence, the child caught fire, and although the flames were extinguished, young Thomas perished two days later. Adam Smith Salt, an infant of two and a half years, also burned to death at home in 1879, with the inquest also taking place at the Crown.

The Crown was not always a peaceable place to drink, as evinced by several police cases. In 1868, landlord Thomas Gardener, appearing before the courts, testified that James Tomlinson had been drunk and disorderly at his pub, which he had entered, offering to fight any man in the place. 'Not finding any person so pugnacious, [he] defied the landlord to put him out, and being so obliged he returned and kicked in one of the panels of the door.' Tomlinson was subsequently fined.

Collier Thomas Green had been drinking in the Crown when he assaulted Ann Sherratt, a servant there, outside the pub in 1870. He walked with her to a lonely part of the road before throwing her down and attempting to take liberties with her. Green was sent to prison for three months. A similar case was reported in 1872, this time in respect of the pub landlord, John Scragg. One afternoon in February, Mrs Scragg went to a funeral in Hanley, leaving her husband at home. While she was absent, Mr Scragg made overtures of an improper character to his domestic servant, Mary Benson, who he kissed several times and acted indecently towards. Mary escaped his clutches, and went and told her mother, with the consequence that Mrs Scragg found out about her husband's licentiousness. He was subsequently fined in court.

A miners' meeting took place at the Crown in November 1882, with Enoch Edwards the principal speaker. He was, by this time, the general secretary of the North Staffordshire Miners' Association and was to enjoy a significant career as a trade union official and MP for Burslem, before his death in 1912. At the Crown, he spoke of the men from the local pits, and 'hoped they would use every effort to build up a strong union at that place'.

Kay Washbrook, writing to the *Sentinel* in 2015, recalled that, during the 1960s, the Crown was run by Reg Leek [or Leeke?], a former miner who had lost an arm in a mining accident. Kay recalled him carrying crates of bottled beer one-handed.

The pub found itself under threat in 1977 when Newcastle Borough Council's action plan recommended that land be developed in Red Street in order to provide 1,400 homes and an increased population of 4,100. History shows that the pub survived but, for a while, Red Street faced the possibility of losing the Crown. Christine Williams, of Liverpool Road, Red Street, told the Evening Sentinel: 'The firm should be compulsorily purchased. This is a community with a lot of old people and many of them like to go to the pub. It is a local community pub and if you take it away you will kill the life of the old people.'

FREEBIRD, Liverpool Road

A much older Duke of York, situated at No. 28 High Street, Newcastle, is listed in *White's Directory* of 1851, though not the Duke of York in Liverpool Road. The latter does not appear in *Kelly's Directory* (1860) either, but it evidently dates from around this time. It appears in brief notice in the local press in August and September 1862: 'TO LET, the "DUKE OF YORK" ALE AND PORTER STORES, Liverpool-road, Newcastle. Apply to Mr. W. R. POPE, next door.'

The Duke of York, which stood on the corner of Liverpool Road and Brindley Street, reappears in the local press in 1874, when two Chesterton men stole landlord William Tattler's cap. (His surname is spelt with only one 't' in some press reports). They were sentenced to a fortnight in prison with hard labour for their troubles. Tattler's attempts to bring greater prosperity to the premises are indicated by a notice he inserted in the local newspapers in August 1874:

To the OVERSEERS of the POOR, and the CONSTABLES of the Parish of Newcastle-under-Lyme, in the County of Stafford.

I, WILLIAM TATTLER, BEERSELLER, now residing at number 54, Liverpool Road, in the parish of Newcastle-under-Lyme, in the County of Stafford, at the dwelling house occupied by me, used as a Beerhouse, and known by the name or sign of 'The Duke of York,' and for six months last past having resided at the same house, do HEREBY GIVE NOTICE that it is my intention to apply at the next GENERAL ANNUAL LICENSING MEETING, to be holden at the GUILDHALL, in the Parish of Newcastle-under-Lyme aforesaid, on the Ninth day of SEPTEMBER next, at 10 o'clock in the Morning, for a LICENSE to sell WINE and excisable LIQUORS by RETAIL, to be drunk or consumed in the house and premises thereunto belonging, situate at Number 54 LIVERPOOL-ROAD aforesaid, and whereof I am the present occupier, and which I intend to keep as an Inn, Alehouse or Victualling house.

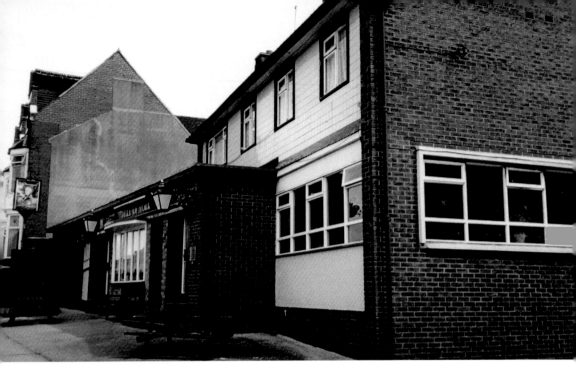

Above: Duke of York, 11 July 1998.

Below: Freebird, 5 May 2016.

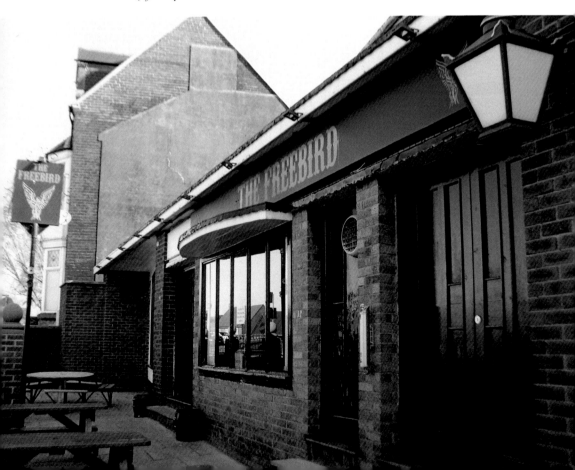

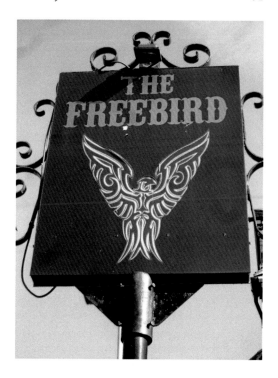

The Freebird sign, 5 May 2016.

Given under my hand this Fifth day of AUGUST, One Thousand Eight Hundred and Seventy-four.

WILLIAM TATLER.

Tattler's application for the Duke of York beerhouse, supported by the signatures of 108 local residents, was considered at the following licensing session at which it was stated that Tattler was contemplating the enlargement of his premises through the annexation of an adjoining house. The application, at this stage, was refused.

Information in Newcastle Library archives indicates that the Duke of York was rebuilt on a nearby site in 1959.

The pub has known many vicissitudes since then. It formerly had a highly attractive and very colourful 'battle' mural on the left-hand wall of the lounge, which was highly praised by CAMRA Potteries in Potters Bar (December/January 2000). It was subsequently sacrificed in a major refurbishment of the pub. A note from the editor (Potters Bar, August/September 2000) explained that the mural had been commissioned by former licensee Ted Bentley in the mid-1960s, but had been in a poor state of repair when a new licensee had arrived in 1999. The note continued, 'The lounge had been closed for many years and considerable redecoration work was required to open it up again. Even so, it was still dull and dreary, and was not very well patronised, so a costly refurbishment plan was undertaken. Unfortunately, the battle mural, in its stained and damaged state would have detracted from the refurbishment, so it has been removed and placed in storage … awaiting a good home.'

So did the Duke of York lose its most attractive – and probably restorable – feature as part of the new refurbishment? Perhaps it remains safely 'in storage' somewhere.

The Duke of York was renamed the Freebird in 2010 after a 1973 power ballad by the American rock band Lynyrd Skynyrd. Among the items found in the pub following its reopening have been picture boards of Kiss band members, a huge Union flag, a bikers' helmet in the style of a human skull and much Americana.

GEORGE & DRAGON, Ironmarket, Newcastle

Information in Newcastle reference library traces the George & Dragon back to 1816 at the latest. A trade directory of 1822–23 lists Mary Shufflebotham, victualler, as keeping the pub.

The pub played host to friendly societies for much of the nineteenth century. In 1833, around 200 members of the Pottery and Newcastle District of the Loyal and Independent Order of Odd Fellows celebrated their anniversary at the George & Dragon, having heard a sermon at St George's Church and processed through the town.

Host Shubottom is referred to in the report of the aforementioned proceedings, and slightly confusingly, it is John Shubotham who placed a notice in the local press in January 1835, announcing his imminent departure for the Wine and Spirit Vaults in Red Lion Square, Newcastle. He thanked the friends and customers who had supported him at the George & Dragon, and recommended his successor, Mr Beech. James Beech also took out a notice in the newspapers announcing his arrival and advertising his 'choice flavoured wines, excellent spirits and good, home-brewed ale'. The commodious stabling at the pub was also mentioned. Beech is duly listed as keeping the George & Dragon, at No. 36 Ironmarket, in a trade directory of 1836.

In 1858, the St George's Dividend Friendly Society lodge of Oddfellows – 'established 40 years ago, holding its meetings at the George and Dragon, Newcastle' – announced its decision to convert into a dividend society. The society continued to meet at the George & Dragon.

The pub was advertised as being for sale by auction in 1877, and particulars give an indication of its desirability. It was advertised as a fully licensed public house embracing a brewhouse, stables, cellaring and enclosed yards, in the occupation of Mrs Evans. Also was added, 'The premises are replete with every convenience for carrying on a first-class business, occupy an excellent and

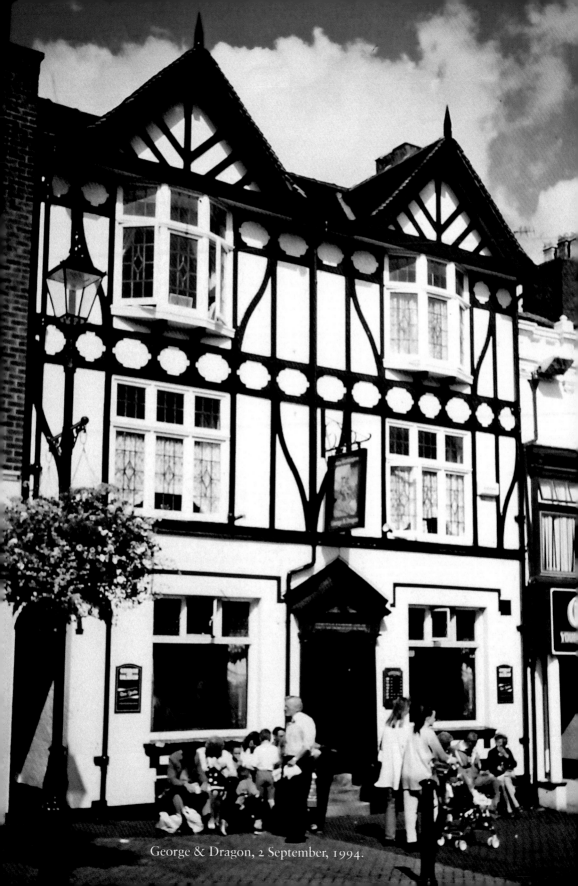

George & Dragon, 2 September, 1994.

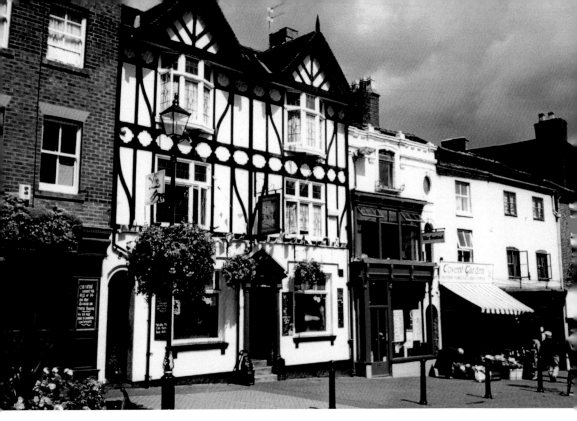

George & Dragon, 13 July 1998.

commanding position, have never changed hands for the past 37 years, and afford a favourable opportunity for a desirable and safe investment ...'

A similar sale notice included in the *Staffordshire Sentinel* in 1887 declared that the George & Dragon had changed hands once in forty-six years.

The pub was known for having a quirky clock in 1981. Both the George & Dragon and the Superstar (now Reflex) displayed clocks with numerals printed the wrong way around on their faces. Joyce Rogers, a barmaid at the George & Dragon, told the local press, 'It causes great laughs. Sometimes people think they will miss their buses or they are too late for a drink until they realise it's a back-to-front clock.'

GOLDEN LION, High Street, Newcastle

A list of past and present pubs in Newcastle reference library gives an earliest discovery date of 1734 for the Golden Lion. A directory of 1822–23 lists Martha Ellerton, victualler, as keeping the pub, while George Titley is listed in 1836 – its address was then given as Penkhull Street. At this stage, it was involved in the business of land carriage in Newcastle, as we note that John Bull's caravan left the Golden Lion every Tuesday en route to Cheadle, Uttoxeter, and Ashbourne. Every Monday night, William Turner plied the route

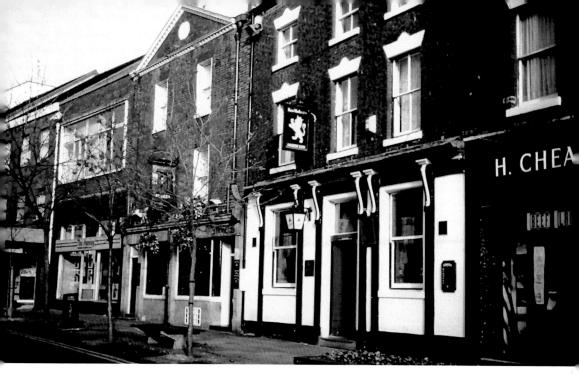

Above: The Golden Lion, 26 December 1996.

Below: The Golden Lion, 5 May 2016.

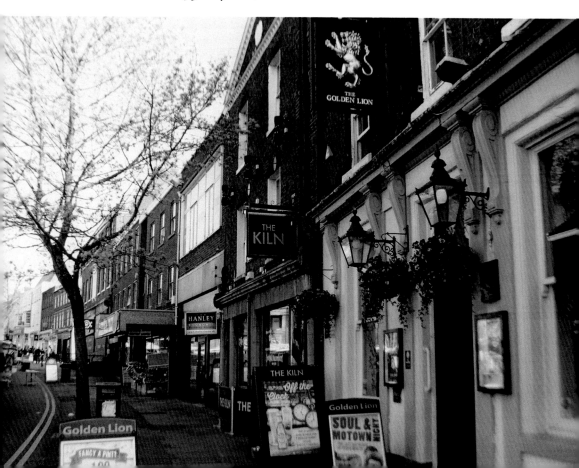

from the Golden Lion to Stone and Stafford. Keeping a pub was sometimes a precarious existence, and landlords occasionally had a secondary occupation. In 1851, Golden Lion landlord Joseph Dierden was also employed as a railway contractor.

References to the pub come thick and fast from early Victorian times on account of the hostelry's centrality and its proximity to the town's market. It was convenient for visitors to Newcastle, as seen from several mentions in the local newspapers. For instance, a case in the police court reports in 1865 referred to a Thomas Bentley, who had brought several persons in a conveyance from Hanley to stay at the Golden Lion Inn. However, when a disturbance broke out, Bentley and his passengers jumped back into their horse and carriage, and Bentley drove off at a furious pace that resulted in his carriage running into a cart, causing damage to his own vehicle. Perhaps other operators ran a safer service. By May 1865, it was announced that an omnibus service from the Golden Lion to Trentham and Tittensor would run every Sunday, leaving the inn at 2.30 p.m. and returning at 6.00 p.m.

The Golden Lion's location in the bustling market town saw it being visited by a wide spectrum of drinkers, some of whom were unsavoury.

In 1872, landlord Francis Dean was summoned for allowing notoriously bad characters to call at his house – to wit, five well-known prostitutes, some of whom were convicted thieves or returned convicts. A fine was imposed. However, a highly unpleasant assault took place in The Golden Lion in 1878, when James Pimlott, a fish-hawker, attacked Abraham Brown, a pointsman. Pimlott came to the house hawking fish, and sold some herrings to two men who were drinking. However, Pimlott, being convinced that he had been short-changed by one of the parties, lost his temper. Brown, who had spoken up for the purchasers, was subsequently knocked to the ground by the fish-hawker, who then knelt on his chest, put two fingers down his throat and two around the root of his tongue, and held him in this position until he became unconscious. He was saved from further damage as his wife alerted the landlord of the pub. Brown's mouth was full of blood, and he suffered from the effects of the injury to his throat for some time afterwards.

Another row in 1881 saw two travelling musicians, who were lodging at the Golden Lion, becoming drunk and disorderly and smashing a window. They were subsequently fined.

A fondly remembered publican is Bill Kirkham, who took over the pub in 1969. Twenty years later, pub regulars fought to save his job when Bass refused to extend his tenancy. He was then sixty-eight years old and had run the pub alone since the death of his wife four years earlier. He was well known in the town. One customer, Paul Jones, told the press, 'If they get rid of Bill, it would be like getting rid of a piece of Newcastle itself.' However, despite a petition and the customers' campaign to keep Bill at the Golden Lion at least until his seventieth birthday, he was forced to leave.

The pub has undergone several major refurbishments since, notably in April 1997 when the interior was drastically altered.

GROVE HOUSE, London Road, Chesterton

In 1971, the Grove House inn was in danger of being demolished, and this threat to its future generated much interest in its past history. It was stated in the press that it was then 'believed to be Chesterton's oldest pub' and that it could be 'traced back by abstract of title to 1855'. Reference was also made to the pub's nickname, the 'Cutting Gleaves', named after a previous landlord. The landlord's surname is spelt as 'Gleaves' and 'Gleeves' within the same news article, suggesting a carelessness on the part of the journalist. It was also claimed that there had formerly been a brook at the rear of the pub – later covered over – and that the ex-landlord would sometimes take a short cut over it, hence the nickname of his hostelry, 'the Cutting Gleaves'. Much of the information contained in the report appears to be based on hearsay, but we can begin to piece together some of the pub's history through some examination of trade directories and the nineteenth-century newspapers.

The name of Thomas Gleaves, shopkeeper, is found in the Chesterton section of *Kelly's Directory* for 1860. He is the only Gleaves recorded in the commercial listings. He is not listed in the commercial section of *Kelly's Directory* of 1872, though Mrs Ann Gleaves, shopkeeper, is. *Keates' Directory* for 1873–74 lists several beersellers – whose premises are not named – as operating in Chesterton, though no member of the Gleaves family is mentioned, and there is no reference to the Grove House.

However, one other source confirms that the Grove House, in its original form, was trading at this time. The following notice appeared in the *Staffordshire Times* in August 1875:

> To the Overseers of the Poor of the Parish of Wolstanton, and to the Chief Constable of the same Parish, in the County of Stafford, and to all others whom it may concern.
>
> I, THOMAS GLEAVES, Beerhouse-keeper, now residing at the Grove House, Primrose Grove, Chesterton, in the Parish of Wolstanton, in the County of Stafford, and for more than six calendar months last past having resided at the same place, DO HEREBY GIVE NOTICE that it is my intention to apply at the next General Annual Licensing Meeting, to be holden at the Town Hall, Newcastle-under-Lyme, in the said County, on the eighth day of September next, for a License to hold any excise License of Licenses, to sell by Retail under the 'Intoxicating Liquor Licensing Act, 1828, all Intoxicating Liquors

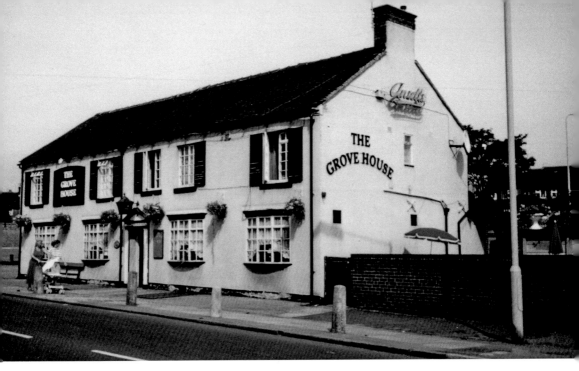

Above: The Grove House, 28 August 1991.

Below: The Grove House, 30 April 2012.

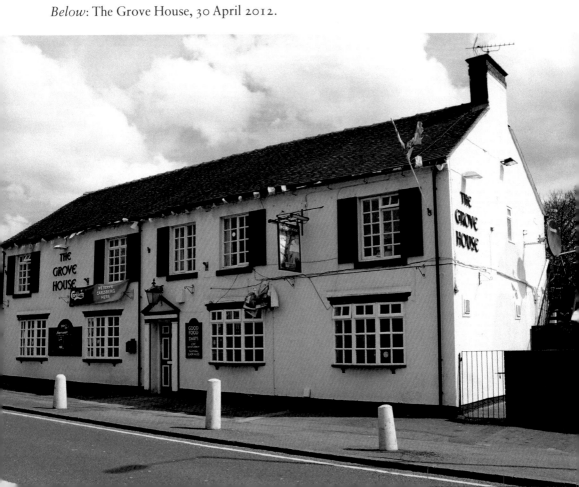

to be consumed either on or off the house or premises thereunto belonging, situate at Primrose Grove, in Chesterton, in the said Parish of Wolstanton, now in my occupation or possession, of which premises John Thorneycroft, of Primrose Grove, Chesterton, Engineer, is the owner, of whom I rent them, and which said house has for three years and upwards last past been used as a Beerhouse.

GIVEN under my hand this third day of August, one thousand, eight hundred and seventy five.

THOMAS GLEAVES.

In September 1875, a report on the licensing meeting for Pirehill North confirms that Thomas applied for a licence for his house at Primrose Grove, presenting a supporting petition of 300 signatures. Unfortunately, further information appears to be in short supply. However, the beerhouse was definitely operating at this time, because later that month the *Staffordshire Times* reported that Thomas Gleaves, beerseller, had been charged with assaulting Eliza Cooke, who had been to fetch a quart of ale for supper from Gleaves. He was reported to have sold her a bottle of ginger beer for a shilling, but upon handing over her change, had kissed her and behaved inappropriately. A witness, Thomas Callaghan, a shoemaker, had seen a scuffle ensue. Gleaves was let off on payment of 8 shillings and costs.

At the time the pub faced possible demolition in 1971, it had been kept by Mrs Claira Kenworthy, aged fifty-nine, and her husband George, sixty-two, who, it was reported, had kept the pub for an impressive twenty-four years. Claira remarked that she had applied for alteration and enlargement of the premises twenty years previously, but that this had been turned down. One recollection of the pub came from Frank Albert Platt, aged eighty-seven, of London Road: 'Everyone had their own seat at the Cutting Gleaves. If a stranger sat at one of the places looked upon as belonging to somebody else, everyone would shout, "Don't sit there. That's ..." and they would name the person who sat there.'

The pub was saved, however, by the Secretary of State for the Environment's decision to exclude it from a clearance and development plan proposed by Newcastle Borough Council. This followed a public inquiry in June 1971 when Ansells Breweries Ltd opposed placing a compulsory purchase order on its premises. The order related to the pub and six adjoining houses fronting London Road. The land was proposed for redevelopment as a car park to be incorporated with other plans including a new community centre. The survival of a pub that still trades today can be attributed to the brewery's stance at this time. Its representative, Mr W. R. Good, told the inquiry that there was no reason why the Grove House could not remain.

It reopened in January 1977, more than twice its original size, the brewery having bought two adjoining cottages. It was completely restyled, inside and out, with ersatz Georgian bay windows. The new licensees were Graham and Florence Richardson, who had moved from the Spring Cottage in Bucknall, and the brewery boldly declared in a press advert, 'Come and see for yourself the pub saved from the bulldozer.'

MUSEUM, George Street

The Farmer's Arms beerhouse was opened by Thomas Hobson around 1841. Hobson appears in the 1851 census, listed as a beerhouse keeper, aged forty-eight. Details from the 1861 census relating to the Farmer's Arms convey that the beerhouse keeper was Joseph Beeston, aged sixty-two.

The name of the present pub can be explained with reference to the enterprise of Joseph Cook, who was certainly keeping the nearby Waterloo Inn in George Street by 1858. Here, he regularly held horticultural exhibitions. Also, by this date, he was able to advertise his 'Museum of Natural History, Curiosities, &c.' in the local newspapers. Visitors to Newcastle Wakes were predictably drawn to Cook's exhibitions, which in 1859 included the following:

A number of birds and animals from different quarters of the globe, which are carefully stuffed and preserved in glass cases. Amongst them are exhibited a few freaks of nature well worth the attention of the curious, viz., a lamb with six legs and two heads, a hen with four legs, a kitten with six legs, a kitten with only two legs, a chicken with four legs and two heads, a kitten with two perfect faces and four eyes, but only one body and four legs. The museum also contains a large and handsome collection of humming birds.

Cook took delight in announcing additions to his collection in the newspapers, and over the course of the next few years, his exhibits included what were advertised as a white starling, caught in the neighbourhood of Keele, an eight-legged puppy born locally and 'a Hen of some organisation, being thoroughly dualistic in all its members and reproductive powers'.

In February 1867, 'Old Joe' Cook announced in the local press that he had opened a 'Museum of curiosities in nature and art' on a new site – that of the present Museum inn in George Street:

Old Joe Cook begs to direct the attention of the public to his unrivalled collection of natural curiosities. Now open to gratuitous inspection in his newly arranged museum, where the Farmers Arms, by extensive alterations, has been made suitable for his valuable collection. The museum contains some of the most extraordinary freaks of nature in birds, beasts and fishes.

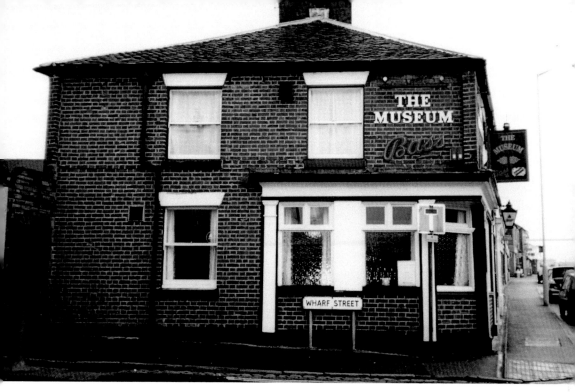

Above: The Museum from Wharf Street, 27 November 2000.

Below: The Museum, 29 July 2013.

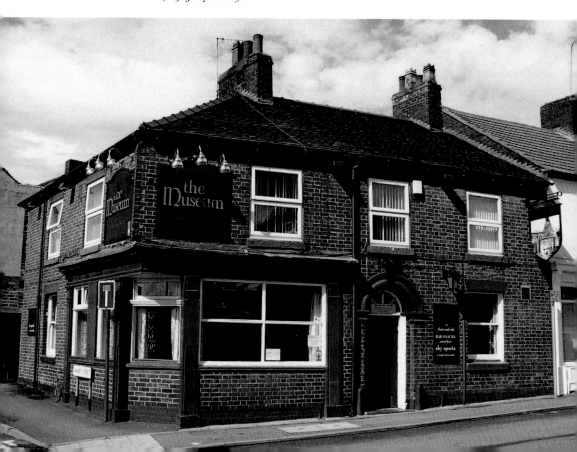

Comprising the largest wolf in England, a beautiful Arctic fox, a lamb with
two heads, six legs and two entire bodies ...

Cook's association with the beerhouse arguably continued for longer than he'd
have wished. He advertised the recently enlarged and improved premises as
to let in 1868, announcing that he was retiring from business. The beerhouse
embraced a large and well-fitted bar parlour, a tap-room and the room that
contained his museum of curiosities. There were also five bedrooms, a rear
yard and a gas-lit skittle alley. There appears to have been no serious interest
in the beerhouse, as Joe found it necessary to place a similar notice in the local
newspapers in April, 1870.

William Bailey was keeping the Museum Inn at the time of the 1871 census,
listing himself as a 'gardener'. It is clear, however, that Cook's curiosities stayed
on the premises, for in late 1872, the 'valuable COLLECTION of STUFFED
BIRDS, BEASTS and REPTILES, belonging to Mr Joseph Cook, who has left
the public business' was being advertised for sale.

The Museum served the community in other ways. In 1868, thirty or forty
employees of the North Staffordshire Brewery of Baker and King took dinner
at the Museum, Cook providing a dinner supplemented by plum pudding and
'a plentiful supply of capital beer'.

The Museum was mentioned in the local police courts in 1885, when
landlord Sampson Fowler was charged with trading during prohibited hours
on a Sunday. Ellen Watkin, aged fourteen, was charged with being illegally on
the premises.

The previously mentioned Waterloo Inn in George Street closed in 1963, but
when this closed, Rex and Audrey Ward removed from the premises to take
over the Museum. Audrey (1921–2003) lived in Newcastle all her life, and met
her husband at a dance at the Castle Hotel in the town; they married in 1947.
In 1983, Rex and Audrey separated, with the latter retiring and moving to
Andrew Place in Newcastle. Audrey died at the age of eighty-one.

In recent years, Chris and Katie Lehanne-Aston left in 1995. The Museum
underwent refurbishment in late 2013.

NEW SMITHY, Church Lane, Wolstanton

The history of this public house has its origins in the growth of Burslem and
Longport following the completion of the Trent & Mersey Canal in 1777, and
the establishment of a new road through the village of Wolstanton shortly
afterwards. Charles Barker, a local shoemaker (he is listed in Parsons &
Bradshaw's 1818 Directory) had a three-sided square of industrial workers'
housing built, just below the Church Cottages. Dating this development is
difficult, although Barker's Square does appear on the 1822 Map of the Parish

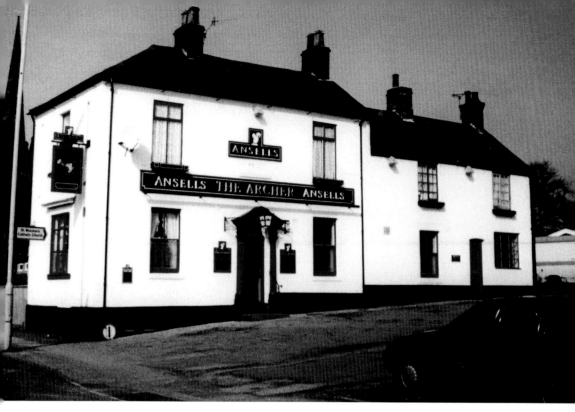

Above: The Archer, 9 March 1993.

Below: The New Smithy Inn, 21 June 2001.

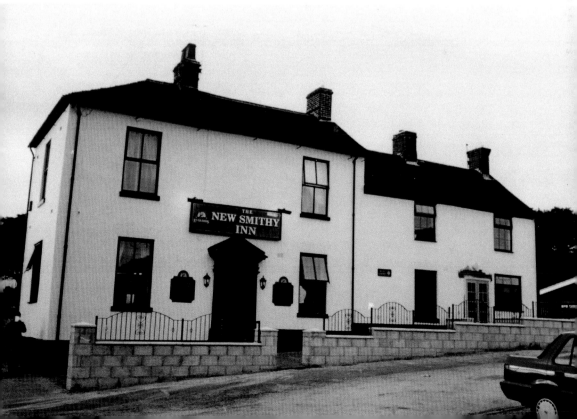

of Wolstanton, and the building which eventually became the Archer public house is reckoned to date back to *c.* 1800–10.

Barker's Square became inhabited mainly by potters and tradesmen working in and around Burslem. There is no reference to a beerhouse in the square in the 1841 census, nor in 1843 when seven dwelling houses in the square were up for auction. However, auction particulars in 1857 reveal that the New Inn beerhouse was occupied by Henry Hackney. Sarah Gettring is listed in *Kelly's Directory* of 1860 as 'beer retailer, Church Street', and in the 1861 census for Barker's Square she is recorded as being aged fifty-three, born in Chell, and keeping a beerhouse. In 1882, auction particulars indicate that the New Inn beerhouse was 'To let ... with large yard, stable and piggeries; rent £25.'

The New Inn was used by patrons of the adjacent Marshlands Picture Hall (1911–60) and by miners from the nearby Wolstanton Colliery (closed 1985). Pub regulars raised money for the North Staffs Licensed Victuallers' efforts for prisoners of war during the Second World War and, in 1951, members of May Bank British Legion held meetings at the pub while more permanent headquarters were being considered.

At some stage subsequently, the pub was renamed the Archer. Former Wolstanton Colliery miner Tim Pattison remembers the pub in the 1970s: 'On a Sunday, when it was 2.00 p.m. closing time, I knew miners who would finish at the pit at 1.45 p.m., throw off their helmets and respirators, sprint up the bank to the Archer, and have four or five pints before going back down to the Pithead Baths, showering, and THEN going home!' [Tim Pattison, taped interview with Mervyn Edwards, April 2001].

The Archer was last refurbished by Ansells in August/September 1992, but was not altered structurally. The room overlooking Church Lane was ultimately occupied by a pool table, (formerly located in the upper section of the pub). A pigeon club's purpose-built structure stood at the rear of the pub, the club itself transferring to headquarters elsewhere following the threat to the Archer's future, which led to the Save The Archer campaign being established in February 1997.

The Friends of The Archer committee, whose spokesman was Terry Fitzmaurice, were able to secure the building's future by persuading Newcastle Borough Council to extend the Wolstanton Conservation Area to include the structure. However, Allied Domecq was determined to sell off the pub and the licensee Pam Leigh closed the Archer on Friday 13 March 1998. A private party took place on the following night, attended by invited guests who were considered by Pam to have been regular patrons of the pub. She remained in residence until 13 May, departing afterwards to run the Lamb in Stoke Prior, Leominster. The Archer was boarded up and all exterior signage removed on 21 May. The purchasers of the building, the Roman Catholic Church, demolished the old pigeon club hut to improve access to St Wulstan's church and parish hall. The building's white exterior survived until June 2000, when the owners repainted it burgundy.

With its exterior newly painted off-white, the pub, incorporating structural alterations, reopened as the New Smithy Inn on June 21 2001.

Old Bull's Head, Lad Lane, Newcastle

The origins of the Old Bull's Head as a public house appear to date back to the seventeenth century.

It sometimes appears in trade directories without the 'old' part of its appellation and its address in some is given as 'Ironmarket'; for example, in the trade directories of 1822–23 and 1836, we find that Edward Cooper, victualler, kept the 'Bull's Head, Ironmarket'. John Plant was keeping the pub by 1839.

Interior interpretation dating from the 1999 refurbishment included an account of a cheating soldier who shot himself dead in the bar of the pub when he found himself at the centre of a love triangle. The date was 1842. However, further tragedy was to occur at the pub in 1861 when John Riley, a former soldier with the 39th regiment, died of a heart attack while talking to landlord John Greaves, who had succeeded George Hubbard as licensee in 1860. Riley had been living on the premises for several months.

In 1871, Greaves announced in the press that he was retiring, having kept the Old Bull's Head for eleven years. He was succeeded by Edward Bentley, who advertised his 'ales, wines and spirits of the best quality'. He also reminded the public that stabling was available and that an ordinary was held at the pub every week on Mondays. Among the groups and societies that met at the pub in the 1870s was the North Staffordshire Licensed Victuallers' Friendly and Protection Society.

The pub has a connection with Newcastle Male Voice Choir, formed in 1943. Don Rogerson recalls that, after rehearsals in the 1950s, the choristers used to visit the Old Bull's Head: 'We had the little back room to ourselves. The friendly landlord was Arthur Cartlidge. We didn't have to fetch our beer. He brought it to us. We used to sing in there and raise the roof.' [Interview with Mervyn Edwards, May 2003].

A bizarre occurrence at the pub was reported in the local press in 1957. An Irishman surprised drinkers in the bar of the hostelry by giving away £1 notes. He gave one man £82 and ordered twenty pints of beer. Shortly afterwards, the police arrived and arrested him on suspicion of stealing £200 in notes from Lloyd's Bank in Newcastle. Newcastle magistrates heard that Patrick O'Callaghan had attempted to escape via the roof of the ladies' toilet in the pub.

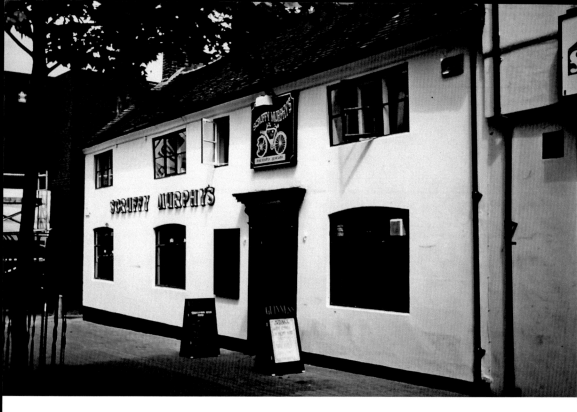

Above: Scruffy Murphy's, 16 July 1996.

Left: Scruffy Murphy's interpretative plaque, 16 July 1996.

SEAN PATRICK MURPHY
Known to friends and strangers alike
as 'SCRUFFY' met and married
Mary O'Brien, the post mistress.
Scruffy persuaded her to enter into
a small business venture allowing
him to sell whiskey & porter in a
shop next door.
The result was a thriving establishment
called 'SCRUFFY MURPHY'S'.
Scruffy emigrated to England during
the potato famine in 1845 Bringing
his little drop of Ireland here to
Newcastle Under Lyme.

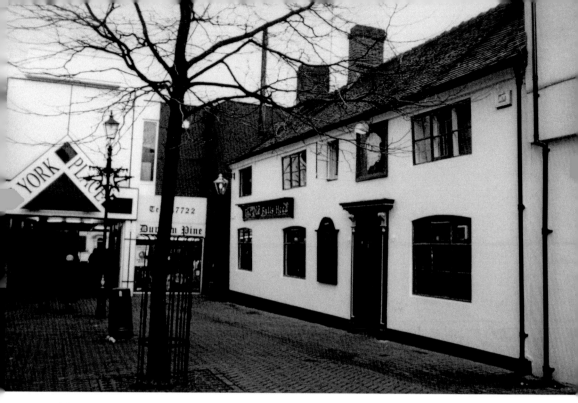

Old Bull's Head, 2 December 1999.

The historic interior of the pub was affected by alterations in 1956, 1968 and 1983. It might well have disappeared altogether in the 1960s on account of the borough council's original plans for the redevelopment of part of the area between Merrial Street and Ironmarket. The county council, however, asked for the decision to be reconsidered on account of the historical value of some of the properties. A Sentinel letter-writer wrote of the pub in 1964, 'The Bull's Head, well-built and preserved, has some delightful timbering and one of the original open fireplaces with ingle nooks.' In 1996, Allied Domecq renovated the Grade II-listed pub and changed the name to Scruffy Murphy's. It continued as an Irish-themed pub until December 1999 when the traditional name of the Old Bull's Head returned. A refurbished interior embraced murals and information depicting aspects of Newcastle history.

Joule's Brewery took over the pub from Punch Taverns in 2012 and reopened on 2 May. It reopened following refurbishment in September 2014 under the direction of a new partnership involving Joule's Brewery and Paul Cope, owner of the Holy Inadequate pub in Etruria.

RED LION, Red Lion Square, Chesterton

According to the research of David Dyble, whose book *A History of Apedale and Chesterton* was published in 2002, the Red Lion is the oldest surviving pub

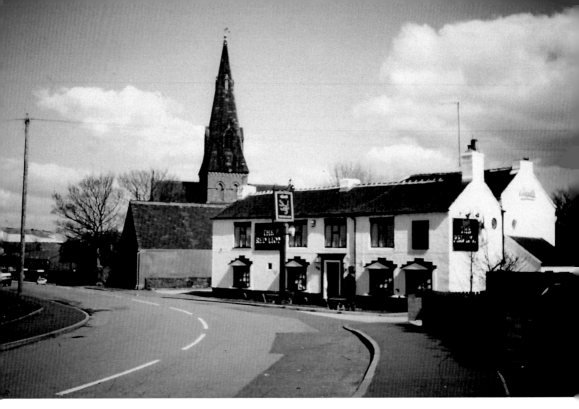

Above: The Red Lion, 10 April 1994.

Below: The Red Lion, 30 April 2012.

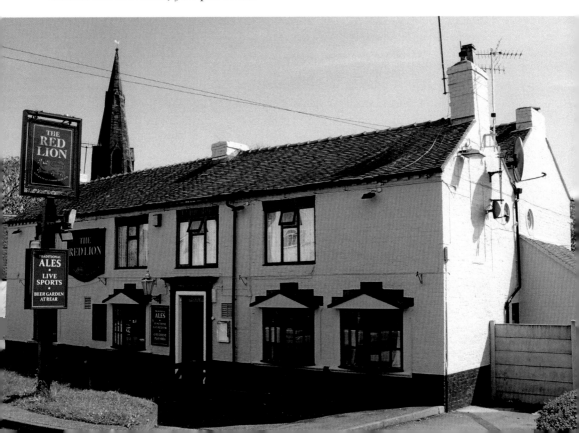

in Chesterton, purpose built *c.* 1750. It was situated at an angle to the original road in order to make it easier for coaches to pull in from the busy road.

J. Smallman, victualler, is listed as keeping the Red Lion in 1818. George Hambleton is recorded as landlord in 1851 and Mrs Ann Hambleton in 1860. Ann was also listed as a shopkeeper.

The Red Lion was able to offer numerous facilities. When it was advertised for sale in 1868, it was described as a 'freehold messuage or dwelling-house (formerly used as a beerhouse, and known by the sign of the 'Red Lion') with the cow-house and stable occupied therewith, situate on the turnpike road leading from Chesterton to Newcastle-under-Lyme'.

Throughout the nineteenth century, the Red Lion was a community hub. Local land was often sold there, as we see in 1837 when landlord Isaac Gibson played host to a sale by auction of land at Hemheath Meadow, which offered a 'superior bed of quarry, tile and brick Clay'. Freehold land at Dunkirk, near Chesterton – and attached houses – was also for sale at the Red Lion in 1862.

It was strongly associated with the Oddfellows Friendly Society, lodges of whom met at the pub, as was often reported in the local newspapers. Their anniversaries usually caught the attention of villagers, with the Loyal Miners' Lodge of the Independent Order of Oddfellows parading around the streets in 1844 and visiting the Methodist chapel prior to taking dinner in the adjacent schoolroom, the food provided by host Hambleton from the Red Lion. At other times, the Oddfellows ate dinner in their lodge room at the Red Lion. The Foresters Friendly Society was also meeting at the Red Lion by the 1880s.

Chesterton's status as a busy industrial village is reflected in the nature of some of the coroners' inquests that took place at the Red Lion.

William Sambrooks, a collier, was killed by a large piece of stone at the Crackley Colliery in 1871. William Rogers, a Chesterton man, was similarly killed by a runaway wagon that hurtled down an incline in the workings of the Minnie Pit at Halmerend in 1885. Joseph Aldridge, who had been missing for eight weeks, was eventually found in February 1887, his body being dragged from a pool belonging to Wooliscroft & Son's brickworks. It was supposed that he had taken this route home as a shortcut, missed his footing and drowned in the water. All the inquests relating to these cases were convened at the Red Lion.

In 1881, the Red Lion found itself competing with a new institution. Chesterton Coffee Tavern was opened in Red Lion Square in a converted shop and dwelling house. It provided food and various entertainment, but no intoxicating liquor, and was aimed at the village's colliers and brickmakers. The 'coffee rooms' are listed in later trade directories as being situated at London Road, certainly as late as 1921.

A CAMRA publication of 1984 mentioned the pub's pigeon and fishing clubs.

RIGGER, Marsh Parade, Newcastle

The story of the Rigger is an interesting tale to tell because it was a creature of its time, created by a society that was throwing off the conservatism of the post-Second World War period and finally letting its hair down. The opening of the pub also has to be examined in terms of its local context too, as it evidently banked on picking up trade from the Crystal Ballroom a few yards away, which had opened in 1958. Another nearby pub, the Shakespeare, had opened in July 1963, with the expressed intention of accommodating patrons of the ballroom.

The circular-roofed new pub in Marsh Parade was opened in October 1963, replacing the Waterloo Inn on the other side of the road. It was named the Bandstand and was said to have 'the unique shape of a rostrum'. The brewery blurb of the day – itself a classic aspect of 1960s-style marketing – remarked that the Bandstand exemplified 'the changing nature of the British inn'. Ind Coope & Co. (West Midlands), in opening their sixty-third new house since 1960, boasted that they were recognising modern development and changes in social taste: 'They realise that the house which cannot offer the public attractive surroundings can no longer expect to do business.' The new pub sold milk, coffee and other soft drinks as part of its brave new world, though its floor plan didn't stray too far from traditional pub arrangements – it had two main rooms, a smoke room and what was known as the band room. Over the bar was a crown, across which was displayed the music of the tune 'A Double Diamond Works Wonders'. The pub's first manager, Stan Perrigo, lived on the first floor in a self-contained flat.

However, in attempting to provide up-to-the-minute catering for the 'in-crowd', the pub suffered the same fate of all similar venues past and present. Contemporary taste is transitory. Only seven years after its opening, the pub underwent a major change.

In 1970, the Bandstand was renamed the Rigger – notwithstanding Newcastle's landlocked location and its virtual absence of maritime history. This was a complete revamp and a time for the marketing people to dream up fresh spiel for a fresh audience. The press advertisement waxed rhapsodic about the nautical theme of the pub – 'launched', it was said, in an informal ceremony. It added that newly appointed manager John Cooper was 'captain' and that he hoped to keep his 'vessel' on a 'very sound and successful course'. There was a battle of Trafalgar mural. *The Newcastle Times* newspaper report ran with the headline of 'Yo, ho, ho at the Rigger', and claimed that the pub was the nearest thing to Nelson's fleet ever to be seen on dry land on account of its internal decoration, embracing 'convincing' cannons, ropes, sails and nautical paraphernalia. It was the concept of local man John Williams. The Ansells pub sold Ansells bitter, Double Diamond and Skol lager. The splash

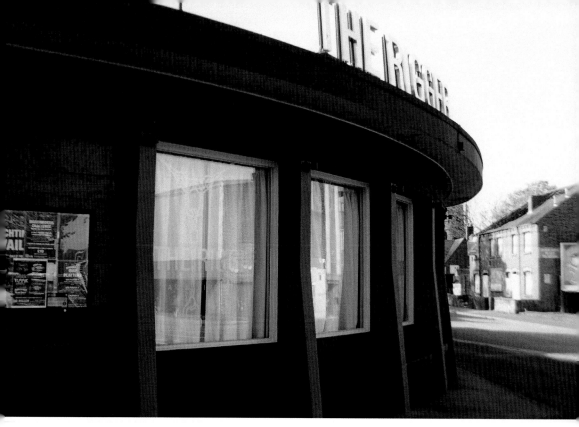

Above: The Rigger, 5 May 2016.

Below: The Rigger, 5 May 2016.

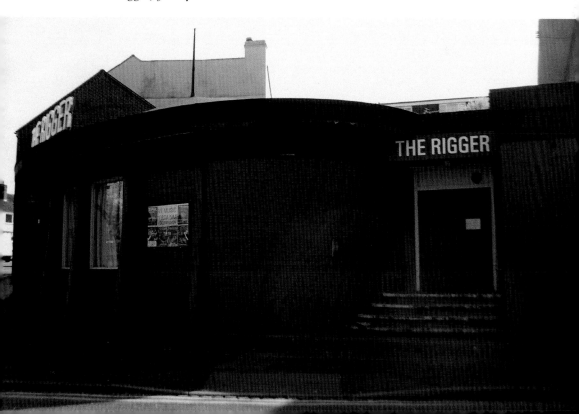

in *The Newcastle Times* exhorted customers to 'Enjoy a hearty tot with old friends in the New Lounge or The Captain's Cabin or in the Rum Cellar, at mid-day you can enjoy a hot or cold snack – nautical style.'

It didn't take too long before the nautical style – and the puns – was sunk. Though the Rigger suffered a major fire in 1991, it has long been known as a successful live music (heavy rock) venue. In 2013, it underwent a £200,000 refurbishment by Punch Taverns, complete with feature walls, band art and skateboards. The present bar counter incorporates four pumps in the style of guitar fretboards and four guitars are placed on a ceiling beam, sensibly out of reach of would-be musicians. The gents' toilet is labelled '*Ozzie's*' (as in Ozzy Osbourne) and the ladies is designated 'Siouxsie's' (a nod to Siouxsie and the Banshees).

ROEBUCK, Dragon Square, Chesterton

We can certainly take the Roebuck back to 1831, for in December of that year, notice was given in the local press of a forthcoming auction to be held at the Crown Inn in Red Street. Among the lots advertised was the Roebuck Inn public house, together with its brewhouse, stables and garden. The premises were described as being lately in the occupation of William Franklin, tenant. The Roebuck was described as being 'well supplied with Water, a new Pump having been put down within a few months. The House is in an excellent state of repair, and the Proprietor has purchased from the late Tenant several useful Fixtures, to prevent the premises being injured, and which will be most advantageous to a coming-in Tenant...'

Thomas Aston is listed as keeping the Roebuck in *White's Trade Directory* of 1851. In 1858, a case of "murderous assault on a police-constable at Chesterton" in the Roebuck was ultimately dismissed. Landlord Henry Mills advertised live pigeon shooting at the premises in 1859, which was followed by a supper for which a shilling was to be paid.

The contents of the public house were offered for sale in the *Staffordshire Advertiser* of June 1861, and they give us some idea of what the interior may have looked like at this time. The sale included:

An extensive assortment of HOUSEHOLD FURNITURE, PUBLIC HOUSE FITTINGS, and other effects, belonging to a person who is retiring from the public business.

Comprising – Tent and iron bedsteads, flock beds and straw mattresses, two handsome boxes of stuffed birds, oak chest of drawers, a 1-pull beer machine, quantity of stillages, skittle frame, pins, and bowls, two dozen spittoons, screens and settles, forms, several large and small round and square drinking tables, cast iron and bright iron fenders, fire irons, jugs and glasses, and a variety of other effects.

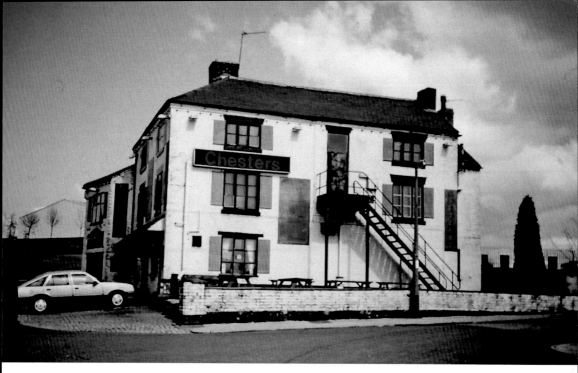

Above: Chesters, 10 April 1994.

Below: The Roebuck, September 2015.

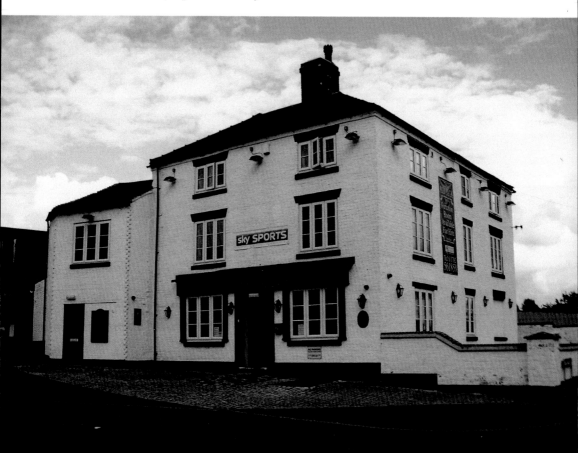

The serviceability of the pub is illustrated through its use as a venue for local business. A coroner's inquest was held at the Roebuck in 1861 following a tragedy at the Milehouse beerhouse, while a sale of property in London Road, Chesterton, was held in 1869.

The Roebuck had many links with the local mining industry. In 1859, four men lost their lives in pits belonging to the Chesterton Colliery, owned by Leighton and Cheadle. The subsequent coroner's inquest at the Roebuck recorded that their deaths were caused by blackdamp (a gas found in mining workings). In 1879, James McCreally, a collier of twenty-seven years, was killed in the No. 1 pit of the Glasshouse Colliery. While working in the pit shaft, McCreally slipped and fell into the sump – which held 6 feet of water – and drowned. The coroner's inquest at the Roebuck gave the verdict of 'accidental death'.

A happier occasion was witnessed at the Roebuck in 1859, when Joseph Heath Esq., of Tunstall, of the Chesterton Mining Co., gave a substantial tea to over fifty of the wives and daughters of his tenantry at the Roebuck. The meal was followed by dancing.

Friendly societies also used the Roebuck, such as the Miners and Blue Tilers Lodge of the Grand United Order of Oddfellows, which processed through the village for its annual festival in 1879, before taking dinner at their lodge room in the Roebuck.

A draft mortgage in the possession of the author is dated 26 April 1900, referring to,

> All that messuage or public house known by the name of the Roe Buck situate at Chesterton in the Coy.of Stafford, Together with the stables, kitchen and cowhouse belonging thereto and now in the occupation of Sarah Jane Hodgkinson and together also with the three messuages or dwelling houses adjoining or near thereto and now in the respective occupations of Charles Hedge and Ellison Hulse ...

The three properties referred to stood on the left of the pub, as indicated on the 1900 Ordnance Survey map. Also in close proximity to the Roebuck were houses in Garden Street and Shaw Street, emphasising the pub's profitable location.

In much later times, the Roebuck Hotel suffered its name being changed to Chesters. It was visited by TV chef Keith Floyd in 2008, who collapsed at the pub, as was reported in *The Sentinel* at the time. The sixty-four-year-old was afterwards taken to the University Hospital of North Staffordshire. It was reported that Floyd was a friend of Chesters' owner Glenn Geldard, and had been staying at the newly refurbished pub. Floyd died in September 2009.

Caldmore Taverns took over the pub in the summer of 2014 and duly relaunched it as the Roebuck in late 2014 under new landlady Sarah Clarke.

VICTORIA, King Street, Newcastle

The premises were erected – probably in the late 1850s – by James Miller in response to the growth of new housing in the vicinity of King Street and possibly in order to attract railway travellers from the new Newcastle station in King Street.

The Victoria was certainly trading as a beerhouse in 1860, as the local press reported on a case of an assault on the premises in June. The assault had been triggered by a dispute involving the playing of cards for ale. Witnesses deposed that a large company was playing and that a 'dozen gallons' of ale were brought in to them. The landlord at the time was John Spencer Graham.

The 1861 census lists Thomas Black, 'tailor and beerhouse keeper' as running the Victoria.

It was Thomas Black, the occupier for nine months, who applied for a spirit licence at the annual licensing meeting for Newcastle in September 1861. This application was opposed on behalf of Mrs Webb of the nearby Borough Arms Hotel. Mr Winstanley, representing Mr Black, stated the case that within the past seven or eight years, 400–500 houses had been erected in the vicinity of the Victoria. Mr Black's house, at that time, contained five rooms on the ground floor, a large yard, a good coach house with an entrance into Miller Street, stabling for three horses and a brewhouse. On the chamber floor, there were seven bedrooms, one of them designated a club room. The licensing magistrates were presented with two separate memorials supporting the application, signed by fifty-eight and seventy-eight people respectively. Among the signatories were the occupiers of Basford Hall and Stonyfields, doctors of medicine, a churchwarden and the High Constable of the Borough. Another supporter was Samuel Hyslop, draper, a future proprietor of the Borough Arms Hotel.

The application for a spirit licence was made on the grounds that excisable liquors were often required in cases of sickness, in which case residents of the new neighbourhood were forced to walk a greater distance to the nearest public house, the Borough Arms Hotel. It was also stated that the Victoria accommodated a different class of customers – i.e., workmen – than the Borough Arms, which was of superior character. Thomas Black himself reasoned that visitors from as far afield as Leek had often inquired about the availability of spirits. They often left their horses with him prior to going into the town of Newcastle. Mr Miller stated that he had spent about £600 on the premises, whose present rental of £28 would be increased if he were to secure a spirit license. The application, however, was refused on the grounds that the existing licences were sufficient for the town.

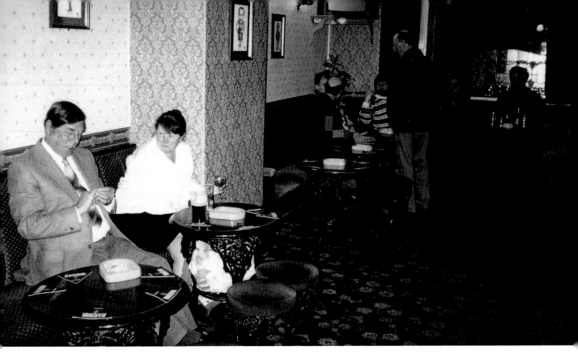

Above: The Victoria lounge, 30 March 1999. The pub was refurbished in 2000, losing its separate bar and lounge.

Below: The Victoria from Miller Street, 5 May 2016.

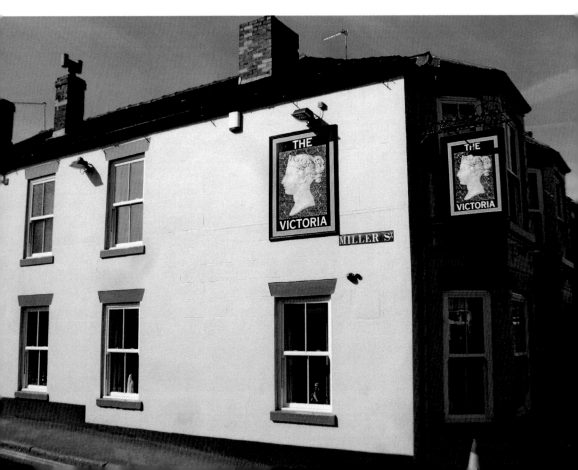

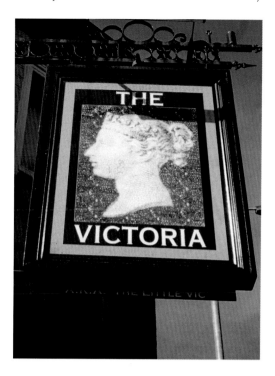

The Victoria pub sign, 5 May 2016.

By the time Mr John Edwards, the keeper of the Victoria at the time, applied for a spirit licence in 1864, Mr Knight, again, opposing on behalf of the Borough Arms, referred to the application as 'a sort of annual thing', and that he had opposed it for 'seven or eight years'. On this occasion, the magistrates granted the spirit licence on the proviso that necessary alterations were made to the accommodation. Edwards subsequently converted his club room into two permanent bedrooms, to the satisfaction of the borough surveyor.

The licence was transferred from the late Mr J. Edwards to his widow in 1867 but the enterprise of Henry Bradbury, described in October 1867 as 'commission agent, &c.' at the Victoria Inn triggered a period of real prosperity. He began to aggressively advertise the premises as being a short distance away from the railway station, promoting its wines and spirits, ales, porter, cider, its food operation and its well-furnished apartments and beds. An ordinary (a meal provided at a fixed time and price) was often advertised, as was the Victoria Inn supper, on Christmas Eve and New Year's Eve, 1869. The food included roast beef, roast turkey, tripe, jugged hare and goose. The advertisements for the Victoria Suppers solicited the 'company of any Gentleman', suggesting that the premises was now attracting a superior clientele than it had at the outset. Henry Bradbury's skill as a caterer led to his being appointed by the corporation to provide refreshments at the Newcastle Smithfield Whitsun Fair in May 1871. By July, he was advertising his 'Carlsberg beer, brewed on the Australian principle by Jacobsen, Copenhagen, also Bass's Pale Ale and D'Arcy's Dublin Stout'. Unfortunately, in the same month, the popularity of the pub got out of hand. The local press reported on antisocial behaviour caused by 'a party of tailors on the spree' in 1871.

In November 1871, Mr Bradbury died suddenly and the licence was subsequently transferred to David Parkinson Norton. It continued to serve the community well, with coroner's inquests and sales of land being held there in the 1870s. Its proximity to the Newcastle railway station was a convenience in 1873, when the employees of the railway in Newcastle held their annual supper at the Victoria. Mr Norton removed to the Vaults in Red Lion Square in 1875.

In more recent times, Clive Hutter, a Somerset man, is remembered as a publican in the 1980s as is the fish tank that he kept in the lounge. The pub at the time ran a fishing club and was popular with teachers from Wolstanton Grammar School.

In 2012, the then derelict pub was purchased by Shropshire-based company Caldmore Taverns and was reopened after refurbishment.

VINE, High Street, Silverdale

The Vine was another Silverdale pub that played host to local friendly societies; for example, in July 1860, the Ancient Order of Forresters held its twenty-first anniversary meeting 'at their new court, the Vine Inn'. The members assembled at noon, and headed by the Silverdale Brass Band, proceeded to the New Connexion chapel where they heard a sermon. Afterwards, the procession took a circuitous route around the village and back to their court where they dined. Mr W. Wrench, who enjoyed a long career as the licensee of the Vine, catered. The Forresters enjoyed food and entertainments at the venue for many years, with around 150 of their brethren being present at the lodge's annual tea in 1897.

The Vine had strong links with local mining. Members of the North Staffordshire Miners Association met in the large room of the Vine in 1863 to discuss trade union activity. The pub accommodated numerous coroners' inquests relating to fatalities in local mines, including the following: George Browning, crushed by in a roof collapse at the Mill Bank Colliery in 1868; Thomas Allman, also crushed by three tons of dirt in a roof collapse at the No. 16 pit of Messrs Stanier & Co. in 1871; and Samuel Shepherd, a furnace keeper who fell and damaged his head at Stanier's ironworks in 1875.

Miners and others sometimes misbehaved in the Vine, the reports of these incidents subsequently appearing in the local press. Seven men, including the notorious Benjamin Hollins, were penalised by the courts for unruly behaviour in 1869.

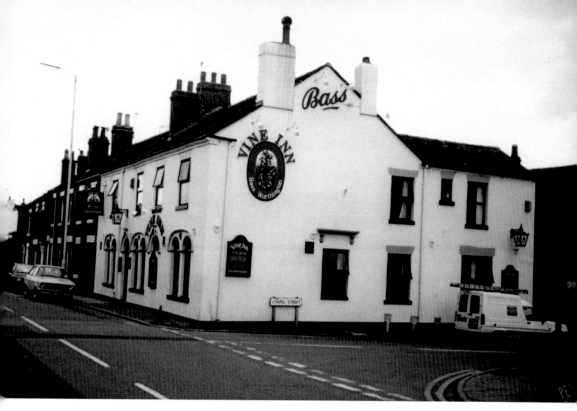

Above: Vine Inn, 29 June 1991.

Below: Vine Inn, 31 May 1994.

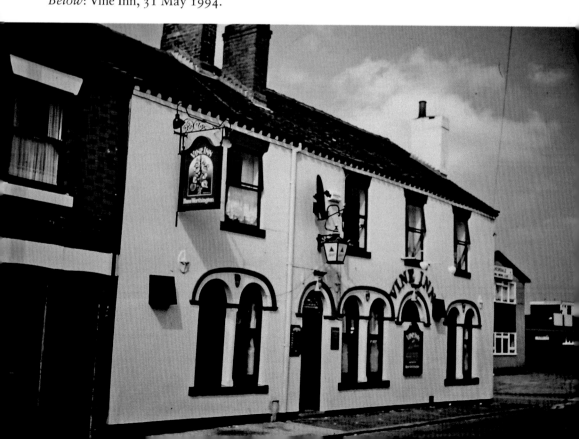

Other groups found accommodation at the Vine. A Conservatives demonstration at Silverdale in 1865 saw over 100 Conservatives enjoying dinner at the pub.

Information on the progress of the Vine and its rivals in Silverdale can often be found in the reports of the annual Trentham licensing sessions. On such occasions, the competitive nature of the business was often laid bare as licensees vied with each other to protect their own interests. A report of the sessions in 1866 recorded that William Wrench – who, it appears, was applying for a full licence – had occupied the Vine for around six years, and had the written support of the incumbent of Silverdale, the curate, the overseers and several respectable persons. However, the solicitor applying on behalf of Jacob Salter, of the Royal Oak, stated that, while not opposing Wrench's application, he wished to show that his client's was the better house of the two. Given the fact that there were plans to establish a much-needed market building for Silverdale, adjacent to the Royal Oak, it was viewed that the pub would become increasingly convenient for visitors to the market and was therefore worthy of a licence. Needless to record, representatives of the Crown, which was, with the Sneyd Arms, the only other fully licensed hostelry in Silverdale, claimed that another licensed house in the village was not required. However, by this time there were 6,000 local inhabitants, and the counter-argument was compelling. So, in the case of the Vine and the Royal Oak, the key issue was whether the two hostelries were adequate enough to be granted the licences. The following was reported:

> Certainly the people might require greater accommodation than two houses could afford, but the Justices were struck with the small class of houses presented to them, both of these houses being in reality very small houses, some 11 or 12 feet square. On this account, they were unable to satisfy themselves that a license should be granted to either of them.

The justices therefore rejected the applications of the Vine and the Royal Oak, but suggested that they would review matters if and when the owners extended their houses and if the promised market building was erected.

At the licensing sessions the following year, William Wrench was able to prove that he had spent £300 on the Vine and had met the requirements of the justices. Meanwhile, the Royal Oak had been built. This time, both applicants were granted a full licence.

Many musical groups were formed in the village, which has a fascinating history in this respect.

The Silverdale Brass Band held its meetings in the Vine. From 1870, they organised a grand annual gala in a field nearby. The band played for dancers and the programme of events would embrace events such as handicap footraces, wheelbarrow racing, hurdle races, Aunt Sally, bag racing, three-legged racing and a pig race. All this was evidently a money-spinner for Mr Wrench, who provided refreshments for the occasions. At the 1874 gala, held in conjunction with Wolstanton Wakes, the band processed from the Vine to the field on each of the event days, and competitors wishing to enter the various races were given notice to apply to Mr Wrench, who also sold tickets for the event. The gala was evidently hugely popular, for it was stated that 'any person detected breaking down the fence will be prosecuted'.

Another musical group attached to the Vine was the Silverdale Choral Society, who held annual dinners there. It was reported that Mr and Mrs Wrench provided the food in 1887. Lest we forget, the renowned Daleian Singers held their inaugural rehearsal in the band room of the Vine in 1957.

A notable licensee was Edward Platt, who died in 1941 having lived all his life in Silverdale. He had been well known in the village as a prominent bowler and an official of the Crown Green Bowling Association. The 'Vine Inn and bowling green' are listed in early twentieth-century trade directories. Silverdale Vine Bowling Club held events at the Vine, sometimes raising money for local hospitals.

WULSTAN, Dimsdale Parade, Wolstanton

The Wulstan was one of a large number of local pubs that opened in 1960. There was a blaze of publicity in the local newspapers, incorporating much brewery commentary that was typical of the time.

The name of the pub, ran the press release, was the old name for Wolstanton. We might respond to this with the following explanatory extract from *Wolstanton: Wolstan's Town* (1908) by P. W. Adams:

> Wolstanton Church is said to have owed its origin to some worthy Saxon of the name of Wolstan (who gave his name to the village), a name borne by several eminent ecclesiastics prior to the Norman Conquest; one of whom was in 1002 Bishop of Worcester. He is said to have been a relative of this parish and a descendant of the Patriarch who gave his name to the village.

The pub, built on former the site of a doctor's residence, was opened by the Mayor of Newcastle, Mr W. E. Welsby. Its leafy surroundings influenced its cottage-style architecture. The Wulstan was designed under the direction of Mr J. A. Dorin of Stoke, and was built by Ind Coope (West Midlands) Ltd. There was accommodation for the licensee, Mr R. C. Thomas, in the form of a three-bedroomed flat with lounge, kitchen and bathroom.

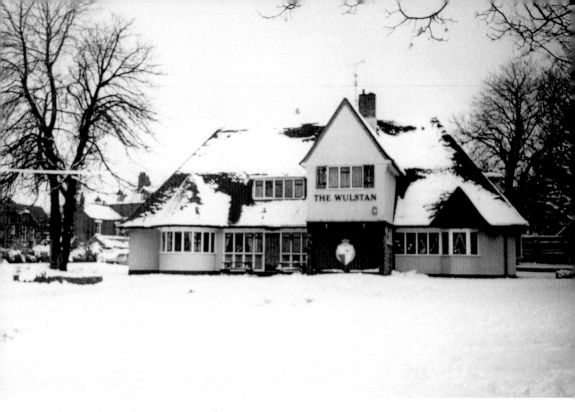

Above: The Wulstan, 9 December 1990.

Below: The Wulstan, 2 March 1994.

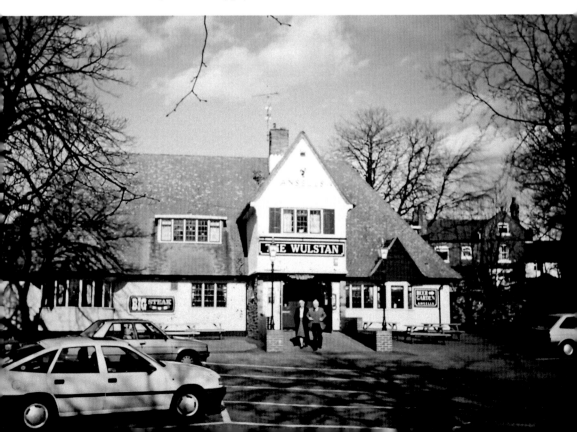

Internally, the pub was built with three bars: the Paddock, which was the saloon bar; the Spinney, which was a lounge; and the Lounge, which, confusingly enough, was a cocktail bar. In the Spinney was a mural panel depicting local buildings and former local residents such as scientist Sir Oliver Lodge. The artwork was carried out by J. Clarkson, the headmaster of Newcastle College of Art, assisted by a master, Mr G. T. Hall. It's worth pointing out that a similar colourful mural depicting famous local figures was produced in time for the opening of the Old Bull & Bush in Hartshill Road, Stoke, in 2015.

The flowery blurb that accompanied the opening of the Wulstan embraced some hyperbole. 'Inside,' the brewery stated, 'it is like being in a country home, with a view from the window of pleasant gardens and trees.' At night, the pub was floodlit from lights arranged in the ambient trees and it also offered a highly attractive beer garden on the extreme right of the building that was a leafy retreat from the sometimes smoky interior. The bluebells will be remembered by many who visited the pub at this time.

Albert and Freda Myatt came to run the pub, and in 1964 Freda launched an over-sixties club, which, by early 1965, had seventy members. In January of that year, the oldest member, Mrs F. Oliver, aged eighty-three, was presented with five bags of coal by Mr George Brayford at a special party. Entertainment was provided by much-loved Potteries comedian Jack Simms, who died in 1976 and is buried in Hanley municipal cemetery. In May 1966, forty members of the club left for a ten-day holiday in Blackpool.

In 1968, the pub, which did food catering for customers and wedding parties, won the *Daily Express* newspaper's 'Pub of the North' competition. At this time, the Myatts' daughter, Yvonne, worked in the pub during the day and modelled in the evening.

Yvonne began a modelling and beauty school at the Wulstan in 1972, by which time she was assistant manageress to her mother. Female customers were instructed on how to apply make-up and false eyelashes and how to exit from a motorcar in a ladylike fashion. Yvonne had begun modelling at the age of twenty-two and she became well known for it in North Staffordshire.

The Wulstan reopened after a total refurbishment on 20 May 1993, its former lounge/smoke room/bar room arrangement having been sacrificed in the interests of an open-plan arrangement. It was also refurbished in 2009.

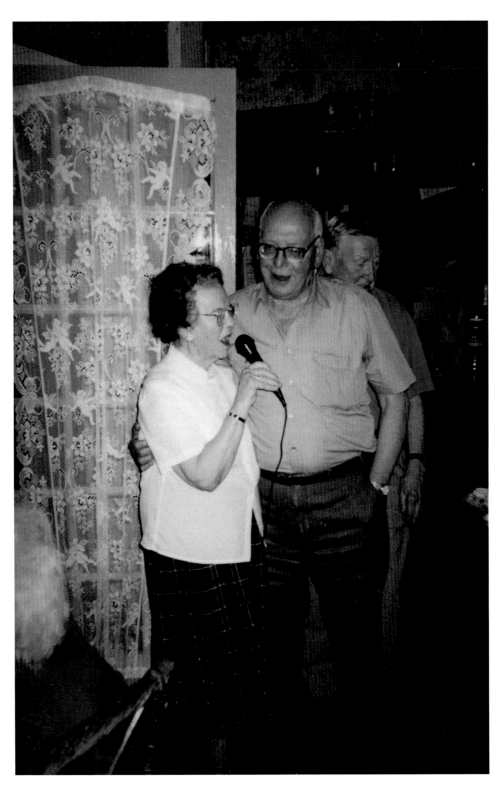

Bill and Hilda.

Acknowledgements

My thanks go to Alan and Linda Massey, Paul Niblett, Cliff Proctor and Gary Tudor.

Every effort has been made by the author to correctly identify copyright owners of the photographic material in this book. If, inadvertently, credits have not been correctly acknowledged, we apologise and promise to do so in a subsequent edition.

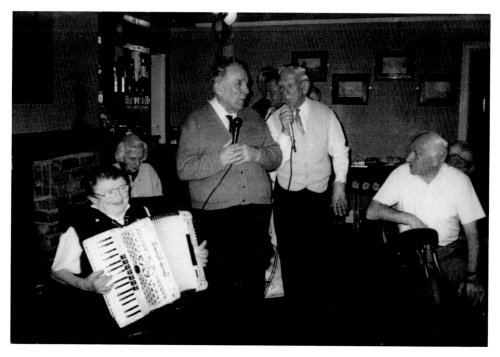

The Greyhound, George Street, 9 February 2002. Open-mic singers. Seated is Jimmy Stockton, then Sam Warrington, Harry Keeling and Roy Evans.

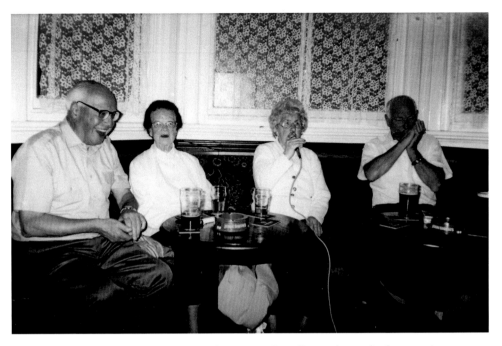

The Bear, West Brampton, 30 September 2000. Roy Evans is on the harmonica.